GETTING
YOUR
BOOK
PUBLISHED

SURVIVAL SKILS FOR SCHOLARS

Managing Editor: Mitchell Allen

Survival Skills for Scholars provides you, the professor or advanced graduate student working in a college or university setting, with practical suggestions for making the most of your academic career. These brief, readable guides will help you with skills that you are required to master as a college professor but may have never been taught in graduate school. Using hands-on, jargon-free advice and examples, forms, lists, and suggestions for additional resources, experts on different aspects of academic life give invaluable tips on managing the day-to-day tasks of academia—effectively and efficiently.

Volumes in This Series

SURVIVAL SKILLS FOR SCHOLARS

GETTING YOUR BOOK PUBLISHED

CHRISTINE S. SMEDLEY

MITCHELL ALLEN

with

HARRY BRIGGS

NANCY S. HALE

CLAUDIA HOFFMAN

C. DEBORAH LAUGHTON

SAGE Publications
International Educational and Professional Publisher
Newbury Park London New Delhi

Copyright © 1993 by Sage Publications, Inc.

For information address:

SAGE Publications, Inc.
2455 Teller Road
Newbury Park, California 91320

SAGE Publications Ltd.
6 Bonhill Street
London EC2A 4PU
United Kingdom

SAGE Publications India Pvt. Ltd.
M-32 Market
Greater Kailash I
New Delhi 110 048 India

Printed in the United States of America

Library of Congress Cataloging-in-Publication Data

Smedley, Christine S.
    Getting your book published / Christine S. Smedley, Mitchell Allen
and associates.
        p.   cm.   — (Survival skills for scholars ; vol. 10)
    Includes bibliographical references.
    ISBN 0-8039-5417-4 (cloth). — ISBN 0-8039-5418-2 (pbk.)
    1. Authorship.   I. Allen, Mitchell, 1951-   II. Title.
II. Series.
PN151.S62   1993
808'.02—dc20   93-11046
                                                             CIP
93   94   95   96   10   9   8   7   6   5   4   3   2   1

Sage Production Editor: Megan M. McCue

Contents

Introduction:

Publishing 101

A colleague at your university sends a proposal to a well-known publisher for a book she wants to write on the meditative tradition in seventeenth-century poetry; about 3 months go by and, following some discussion with the publisher, she is offered a contract. Within the year your colleague gets tenure.

Meanwhile, you have a brilliant concept for a book based upon research you have been conducting. Your ideas are, let's admit it, original, insightful, and definitely significant, and you're positive that nothing remotely similar has been done before. Obviously, any publisher would want to snap it up. You call your colleague and get the name of her publisher, write a brief letter, attach a preliminary table of contents, and send it off. About a month later you get the "Dear John" letter of publishing: "Thank you for considering Publisher X. Unfortunately, your proposed manuscript does not fit our current publishing program." Which doesn't tell you very much of anything. Like why your colleague's proposal was accepted so readily while yours, just as deserving of publication, was rejected.

Like countless others you may find baffling the process by which publishers decide what to publish and what not to publish, but you plunge into the unknown and hope for success, keeping your fingers crossed until you hear from the prospective publisher. Allow us to give you a hint as to why you fail: Crossed fingers have nothing to do with getting published.

While publishing is not always what one would call a rational activity, there *are* specific guidelines you can follow to increase the chances of having your proposal accepted. These guidelines stem from an understanding of the culture of publishing. If you're an anthropologist, your research involves exploring the culture of a specific group; if you're a program evaluator, you recognize that a program is affected by the culture of the organization implementing that program. Similarly, once you grasp the basic culture of publishing, you will more clearly understand what publishers want and thus be more easily able to provide it. And that is why we wrote this book: to give you an insider's view of publishing and thereby help you get published.

We cannot guarantee that, by following the recommendations in this book, every proposal you write will automatically result in a contract; however, the chances are greatly increased that your proposal will not be relegated to the stack of accumulating unsolicited manuscripts (in publishing vernacular, the infamous slush pile), but will land on the editor's desk and thus get the attention it deserves.

So who are "we"? How can we help you accomplish your goal of getting published? This book was written by members of the Editorial Acquisitions and Production Staff at Sage Publications, Inc. Collectively, we represent more than a half century of publishing experience. We have worked in many of the different types of publishers—scholarly, professional, text, trade. We have held positions ranging from sales representative to director of marketing, from editorial assistant to contracts administrator to executive editor. We have given many workshops on book publishing for universities and professional societies. Finally, most of us have been through the process of submitting and getting published a variety of articles, short stories, poems, scripts for educational television, and, yes, books. We've been on both sides of the publisher/

author relationship. And we want to share what we have learned with you.

We were each responsible for writing specific chapters, but, additionally, everyone contributed to the book as a whole. Every editor has his or her own stock of anecdotes—some humorous, some poignant, all enlightening. So the final product is a joint effort, the result of our combined years of experience.

But even this wealth of experience cannot be distilled into a volume this brief. The publishing world is just too vast, too diverse. Writing a nonfiction best-seller that will appear in your local supermarket and airport and land you a guest spot on *The Oprah Winfrey Show* is a much different process from wanting to develop an introductory Western Civilization textbook for the class you have to teach next fall, or wanting to get your dissertation into print to show that 15 years of graduate training were not wasted. The process is different enough that we cannot provide specific advice to cover all eventualities.

So we have decided to focus more narrowly on the kind of book that most scholars write most of the time—the scholarly monograph, edited volume, or advanced text. In the publishing industry, these come under the category of "professional/scientific" books, distinguished not only by the sophistication of the ideas and writing, but also because they are generally sold directly from the publisher to the customer by direct-mail solicitation. Much of the advice offered here also applies to other kinds of publishing, but there are some differences in other types of book publishing that are beyond the scope of this book.

Description of the Book

What exactly do we cover? One of the first facts of life that you, as a prospective author, must face is that publishing, whether scholarly or any other, is not a philanthropic endeavor.

Publishing is a business, and as such, publishers have to make money to stay in business. So in Chapter 1 Christine Smedley covers the business of publishing, including a description of the different types of publishers and the economics of publishing. Such facts will help you understand why you need to approach a publisher with specifics that will help them make a business decision. They will also help you understand that a rejection might not reflect upon the worth of your idea, but rather on the financial constraints or specific needs of that particular publisher.

One of the problems editors face daily is having to tell a hopeful author that his or her concept is not adequate for the basis of a book, that the idea is not worthy of being a book. In chapter 2 Christine Smedley and Mitch Allen help you decide whether your idea is the germ of a book or of one or two journal articles. The chapter gives you direction for making decisions such as whether it is worth turning that dissertation lying on your shelf into a book, whether you should author or edit a book, and how you can actually get down to the business of writing.

Once you have decided what your book is going to be, what subject it covers, and for what audience you are writing, you can start looking for a publisher. In "Finding the Right Publisher" Mitch Allen shows the similarities between the process of looking for an appropriate publisher and the process of doing research. With some targeted fact-finding, you can usually uncover what kinds of books a specific publisher is looking for and whether your book will fit its program, thereby at least eliminating the type of rejection letter referred to earlier—"Your proposed manuscript does not fit our current publishing program." Mitch advises you to think about what you personally consider important when choosing the right publisher—money, prestige, production quality, or marketing expertise. Once you have developed a list of prospective publishers, is there a specific time when you should first contact them? Should you call, write, just send the manuscript?

And what about an agent? Mitch answers all these questions for you.

In the following chapter Mitch shows you how to develop an effective book proposal. Although many publishers have their own proposal guidelines, most cover the same major points—intellectual contribution, market potential, book specifications, author qualifications, and a proposed outline.

So, let's say that you have researched the appropriate publishers, written an outstanding proposal, and sent it off to the first publisher on your list. What can you expect next? Christine Smedley covers the review process that your proposal will go through, what the reviews mean, and how the publisher uses them to decide whether to publish your book. Christine suggests how you can influence the process to your advantage and, if the decision is negative, even benefit from that rejection.

Of course, we hope the review stage will lead to your receiving a contract in the mail; now what on earth does that mean? Unless your contract contains unusual clauses, you needn't run to a lawyer to decipher the legalese. In "The Publishing Contract," Nancy Hale explains the various sections of a standard book publishing contract. What rights does the publisher expect to obtain? What rights do you as author retain? What are the legal responsibilities of both parties, and what royalty is the publisher really offering you? Equally important, what sections of the contract can you realistically negotiate?

Most authors conclude that once they have signed the contract, their contact with the press ends until they submit a final, polished manuscript. Our experience, however, is that authors who build close relationships with the publishing staff along the way are more likely to ensure that their books get the attention they deserve from the publisher.

For example, what about your editor? What kind of help can you anticipate? Harry Briggs describes what you can expect from your editor and how you can use him or her to help develop your manuscript, guide it through the production process, and assure effective marketing. He also addresses the question of what happens if your editor (God forbid!) leaves your publishing house.

In the following chapter, Claudia Hoffman demystifies the production process. Claudia explains what happens to your manuscript during production, what tasks are likely to be your responsibility, and how you can avoid production difficulties.

Now that your book is actually published, will it sell? C. Deborah Laughton provides a realistic assessment of what you can expect from your publisher, in terms of marketing, and what you can do to help promote your own book.

The next chapter, written by the entire writing team, advises you on what to do when things go wrong. Murphy's Law says it will. (Murphy *was* a publisher, you know.) There are a few problems that crop up often in the publisher/author relationship, and these are addressed here. Finally, in the Conclusion we give a brief overview of what we consider the most important lessons we hope you garnered from reading this book.

Throughout the book you will find one consistent theme: Publishing is not only a business, it is a collaborative venture. We have found over the years that the best books are often the result of a close partnership between author and publisher in the persona of the editor. The author dreams of writing a book that makes an unique contribution to human knowledge, and the publisher dreams of publishing such a book. Working together, you and your publisher can make that dream a reality.

Summary

Why did your colleague's proposal get accepted, and yours didn't? She approached the right type of publisher for her book and proved to that publisher that her proposed book would be a solid venture. Once you understand that, we believe that you will be one step closer to getting that contract for your book.

We wrote this book to let you see the inside of publishing, what publishers and editors do, and how they think. Look at it as a mini-research project. By reading this book and following our suggestions, you will be well on your way to joining your colleagues who can proudly point to their books in the university bookstore.

And remember, publishers need you just as much as you need them. After all, they have to publish books to stay in business. And, when all is said and done, publishers and editors love good books. If they didn't, they would be in a more predictable business.

1 | The Business of Publishing

At times we all labor under the delusion that we live in an altruistic world, then something happens that awakens us to reality. Like having your well-written, well-researched monograph on *The Political Views of the Amish* rejected by 10 publishers in a row. Why, you ask; surely this is good research and important information.

Before you begin to doubt your intellectual acumen, bear in mind that publishing is a business. And let us emphasize that publishing is *big* business. In 1992 more than 44,000 titles were published in the United States, with total sales of more than $13 billion (and they say Americans don't read anymore). One Dutch company, Elsevier, which owns such American publishing companies as Springhouse, Congressional Information Service, and Greenwood Press, as well as England's Pergamon Press, had sales of $1.122 billion in 1990. During the same time period, Simon & Schuster had sales of $1.32 billion and Time Warner had $1.14 billion. Such revenue attracts the attention of other businesses, and today many publishing companies are a part of *Fortune* 500 conglomerates, including such communications empires as Harcourt Cinema, Paramount, News Corporation International, and Thompson.

The editor of a small press once remarked, "Publishers exist to make money and make money to exist." The primary purpose of publishing, like any other business, is to generate money. Whether commercial or nonprofit, whether part of a large business empire or a small independent company, publishers need to make money to stay in business, which means they have to sell books. Similarly, if editors don't sign books that make money, they'll end up looking for a new job. R. P. Ettinger, the co-founder of Prentice-Hall, put it succinctly when he said, "A good book is one that sells."

Types of Publishers

Like many other businesses, publishers tend to specialize. And, while publishers come in many sizes, shapes, and colors, they can be divided into three general types: trade book publishers, textbook publishers, and specialized publishers (see Table 1.1). The last includes professional/scientific publishing, the subject of this book. The different types of publishers are distinguished not by the types of books they published, but by the mechanisms by which they sell their books.

Trade book publishers, who account for 25% of book titles published in the United States, market books aimed at the general public. These are the books you will find in chain bookstores like Waldenbooks or B. Dalton, in supermarkets and airports; hear about through the mass media; see their successful authors on lecture tours and television talk shows; and read reviews of in *The New York Times*. To get bookstores to carry their latest offerings, trade book publishers hire sales representatives who call on bookstore managers and buyers to convince them to give their titles some of the store's limited shelf space. We all know the giants of trade publishing: Simon & Schuster, Bantam, Doubleday, Dell, HarperCollins, Random House. And we'd all like to be one of their hot authors; but unfortunately, that isn't likely, even for most professional writers.

Within this group of trade publishers, some "serious" trade publishers, such as St. Martin's Press, Basic Books, and The

Table 1.1 Three Types of Publishers

Trade Books
Customer: General public
Distribution channel: Bookstores, other retail outlets
Distribution mechanism: Sales force plus advertising in general media
Characteristics: Require large print run and sales, media blitz, short shelf life

Textbooks
Customer: Students
Distribution channel: College bookstores
Distribution mechanism: Class instructors, reached through sales representatives, direct mail, advertisements, telemarketing, and other means
Characteristics: Require giving away many free copies to professors; success comes through multiple editions of book

Scholarly/Professional Books
Customer: Scholars, professionals, advanced students
Distribution channel: Direct to customer
Distribution mechanism: Direct mail, advertisements, conventions
Characteristics: Tend to be specialized and have modest sales, often many years in print

Free Press, publish books for the educated public at large. These publishers might well be ones that you, the academic author, deal with during your career. Simon & Schuster, for example, published Bloom's *Closing of the American Mind,* and William Morrow published Deborah Tannen's *You Just Don't Understand.*

Trade books tend to have a short life. Last year's hardcover best-seller is this year's paperback and next year's out-of-print title. They are reliant on extensive advertising and publicity just prior to and just after publication, and only rarely do they stay in print for a long time. Thus, few books of long-lasting scholarly merit end up following this route.

Even so, many scholars dream of writing a popular "crossover" book that will be read by the educated lay public as well as scholars and researchers. Scholarly books, however, are usually on very specialized topics and are bound by the language of the discipline. For a scholarly book to have a chance in the trade market, the author must have something significant to say to those outside the specialty, cultivate a distinctive point of view, and be willing to broaden the subject and substantially modify the tone and language for the lay public. For example, we just mentioned Deborah Tannen. Her first book, *That's Not What I Meant!*, went through four complete drafts before publication. She called the experience her "four-year nightmare," and after all that, the book received only two reviews, one which completely belittled it. For every book that makes it that far, many more disappear immediately upon publication, or never even make it through production.

Textbook publishers are usually divided into two separate divisions in large companies: elhi (kindergarten through 12th grade) and college. Between them, they account for another 25% of books published. In college textbook publishing, the end customer is the student who buys textbooks from the college bookstore. But the *sales strategy* is not geared toward the end user. Rather, college textbook publishers are defined by the fact that they focus on convincing the instructor of a course to assign a particular book and require his or her students to purchase it. (The process in elhi publishing is very different and beyond the scope of this book.) To reach these professors, college textbook publishers use college sales representatives, direct mail, conventions, journal ads, telemarketing, and a variety of other mechanisms. They regularly send sample complimentary copies of texts to instructors who teach the courses they are targeting. These companies may sink hundreds of thousands, even millions of dollars, in developing and marketing a text for, say, the Introduction to Psychology course, and expect to sell tens of thousands of copies. Because of the huge investments such publishers incur, including the high overhead for employing developmental editors, designers, and a sales force, it would not be feasible for them to publish a book destined to sell only a couple of thousand copies. Often, these large books do not make a significant profit until they have gone through multiple editions.

Writing a successful basic textbook takes a special kind of talent, in some ways not unlike the ability to communicate to lay people required in trade publishing. As the author of such a text, you must have, in addition to a strong sense of pedagogy, a clear command of the field at large and be able to articulate it clearly and at a level appropriate for the student. You would be helping students understand your discipline, but you would not be advancing the scholarly basis for your discipline by pursuing cutting-edge concepts. And, if the text is successful, you could find yourself devoting much of the rest of your life to working on subsequent editions.

Specialty publishers can be characterized more by their diversity than by their similarities. They specialize in anything from regional history books to religious treatises, from how-to manuals to professional books. Scholarly or professional publishers and the university presses, the subject of this book, fall in this category. These publishers are characterized by the fact that they sell directly to the end user, rather than through such intermediaries as a bookstore or a professor. Because they publish books aimed at a well-defined audience, they seldom place books in general bookstores (though their titles often appear in university and specialized bookstores). Rather, they can market their books most efficiently and effectively through direct-mail solicitation to the targeted groups that are most likely to buy books on that topic, be they business managers, social workers, or political scientists. Mailing lists can be rented from professional organizations (such as the American Psychological Association or the Academy of Management), from journals and other subscription publications, or from other publishers or professional mailing list brokers.

As we have already noted, scholarly books, such as you are most likely interested in writing, have a definite audience—scholars and researchers interested in your topic. Hence, specialized publishers are the most appropriate choice to reach that audience.

University presses differ from commercial scholarly publishers primarily because they operate on a noncommercial basis and often have some of their costs underwritten by sponsoring institutions, foundations, or endowments. More so than commercial publishers, they can—and are expected to—publish books that are destined to sell few copies but have long-lasting scholarly merit. But even university presses cannot drown in red ink, and, in an age of declining university funds, many university presses are receiving less (occasionally *no*) institutional support. Under those circumstances, commercial considerations increasingly shape their publishing decisions in the same way they constrain the choices of commercial presses.

Like any typology, this tripartite division of book publishing is drastically oversimplified. Serious trade books—from *The Autobiography of Malcolm X* to *In Search of Excellence*—are staples in classrooms and grace the book shelves of many scholars, who might have been solicited to buy via direct mail. Some very influential scholarly books are the products of textbook publishers. Nor do some textbook houses, intent on developing a comprehensive list of books in their more important disciplines, shy away from publishing supplemental textbooks or graduate-level textbooks indistinguishable from the products of scholarly publishers.

Similarly, a large percentage of university presses consider trade book publishing as part of their mission. In modest cases, this is limited to publishing books on regional history and culture. In more extreme cases, university presses aim for the best-seller list. For example, one of the top 50 selling nonfiction books of 1992, along with Princess Diana's biography and Madonna's *Sex*, was University of Chicago Press's *Young Men and Fire*, by Norman Maclean. And serious scholarly and professional books, whether from commercial or university presses, are ubiquitous as textbooks in advanced courses and as supplemental texts in lower-level ones.

While these three types of publishers do overlap to a degree, and while as a scholarly author, you might write for each type during the course of your career, most academic authors write for scholarly/professional publishers most of the time. And the process of finding a publisher, getting a contract, writing a manuscript, and marketing the book are slightly different among the three types. So let's focus now on how a scholarly/professional publisher decides whether your book will be profitable.

Economics of a Scholarly Book

Publishing must be a profitable business. Why wouldn't it be, considering the money they make on your book? After all, you get only a measly 8% in royalties; what do they do with the other 92%?

Very little of that 92% ends up as profit to the publisher. First, costs for copyediting, typesetting, printing and binding, even shipping to and from the warehouse must come out of the publisher's pocket before a book can be sold, costs that are continually escalating. Then marketing expenses must be added in. Direct mailings, journal advertisements, brochures for you to distribute at seminars, convention expenses, all must be paid for. In addition, any business must meet its overhead expenses—everything from salaries to copy machines, typewriters, paper clips, mailing costs, rent or mortgage payments, heating and air-conditioning bills. These and other expenses must be covered before the publisher can speak of a profit. Table 1.2 gives you a hypothetical profit and loss calculation for a typical scholarly hardcover. If the publisher wants to produce a paperback, the number of copies it needs to sell to make the same profit are about triple the amount indicated here.

A typical scholarly hardcover of 320 pages published in the early 1990s might cost, say, $45 for you to purchase; and the publisher might expect to sell 800 copies worldwide. Is this a profitable book? Let us look at some of the elements a

Table 1.2 Profit and Loss Calculations for a Typical Scholarly Monograph

I. Income		
Hardcover sales		
800 copies at $45 list price	$36,000	
Less average discount (30%)	$10,800	
Total:	$25,200	
II. Costs		
A. Production costs (320-page book)		
Design	$800	
Editing ($10/page)	$3,200	
Typesetting, proofreading ($10/page)	$3,200	
Subtotal:	$7,200	
B. Printer costs (paper, printing, and binding)		
Hardcover (1,000 copies)	$4,225	
C. Royalty to author (10% of net sales)	$2,520	
D. Marketing costs		
15% of net sales	$3,780	
E. Overhead costs		
25% of net sales	$6,300	
Subtotal:	$16,825	
Total Costs:		$24,025
Publisher's Pretax Profit:		$1,175
		(4.7% of net sales)

scholarly publisher might examine in analyzing the profitability of this book.

Income. One of the first things a publisher does in evaluating a book proposal is to estimate the probable sales and calculate the income that can be expected, given different selling prices. Obviously, the fewer prospective buyers there are for a book, the higher the price will have to be to cover the publisher's expenses. Will your monograph on *The Political Views of the Amish* sell only 800 copies? While some scholarly books will sell 80,000 copies, and some 80, this is a common sales figure for a focused research monograph in the 1990s. In earlier decades the sales forecast might have been somewhat higher, but university libraries—a key market for scholarly books—no longer have the funds to purchase all the volumes they would like (for example, between 1981 and 1991 the University of California, Berkeley, library purchases fell from 83,000 to 42,000 a year). And this book, like most scholarly monographs, will have a limited audience among fellow specialists who are interested in its topic. Nor will there be many classroom adoptions for such a narrowly focused work. So 800 copies is probably realistic. Of the remaining 200 copies printed, some are given away to you as the author, to book reviewers, indexing services, or professors who adopt your book for class. The rest may end up being pulped for their paper value in a few years.

Eight hundred copies might still sound meager to you, but even though you hear mostly about those million-selling books on the best-seller list, the average sales of a book in the United States is 4,000 copies. This includes everything from monographs on the Amish to Stephen King's latest best-seller or *Scarlett*, the highly touted sequel to *Gone With the Wind*. Which means a *lot* of books, including specialty books such as yours and most trade books, sell a *lot* less than 4,000 copies.

Discounts. While the publisher might sell 800 copies, its income will be far less than $36,000 ($45 × 800); only rarely does the publisher collect the full list price of a book. In fact, the average discount on a book sold by a scholarly publisher will run upwards of 25% or 30%. Most publishers allow their authors to buy copies of their books at a substantial discount, often 40% or 50%; wholesalers who service most university libraries will demand hefty discounts (30% to 35% is not unusual); college bookstores also get a price break to carry your book; and the publisher's marketing department might try to spur individual sales by regularly offering your book in catalogs at a discount of 10%, 20%, or more to individual purchasers. For the purposes of this hypothetical book, we are guessing an average 30% discount, so that the publisher's overall income is $24,200.

Production Costs. Production costs are assigned to individual books, based upon the amount of time it takes for the copy editor, typesetter, and proofreader to work on that book. Copy editors, typesetters, designers, and proofreaders often work on a free-lance basis for a publisher and are paid by the job or by the hour. If these production people are part of the publisher's staff, a certain percentage of their time will be costed to each individual book. Editing costs can vary widely, depending on the location of the press, the extensiveness of the copyediting, the nature of the free-lance market, and other factors. We will fix a hypothetical cost of $10 per page, though the cost could be either half or double that. Similarly, typesetting costs will vary widely, based upon location, the level of technology of the press, the use of either desktop or traditional typesetting technology (see Chapter 8), the use of either free-lance or in-house staff. We will again arbitrarily fix a $10 a page figure on this cost.

Printing. While many publishers have staff copy editors, typesetters, and proofreaders, very few print their own books. The paper, printing, and binding costs of an outside printer will fluctuate with the market, with the type of paper and cover used, with the distance shipped from the printer to the publisher's warehouse, and, most important, with the number of pages in the book and the size of the print run (number of copies printed). The figure given here is a current one for the hypothetical book we are describing. In all, the printing bill generally represents only about 10% to 15% of the overall cost of the book.

Royalties. The royalties paid to authors also fluctuate on scholarly books. Some worthwhile books with a very small potential market might be published on a no-royalties basis, while a potential "best-selling" scholarly book could earn as much as 15% in royalties. Most scholarly books run in the 5% to 10% range. Publishers generally calculate royalties in one of two ways: on gross, or list price, sales (number of copies sold × list price), or on net sales (amount of cash actually received). We've calculated this particular book at 10% of net sales.

Marketing. The publisher must allow a certain amount of money to cover its costs in promoting the book. Different publishers will calculate this cost differently. Indeed, it might differ from book to book within the publishing house. A book such as *The Norton Reader,* with the potential to be adopted in thousands of undergraduate literature courses, will warrant more money spent on promotion than a specialized mono-graph for which there are only a few small graduate seminars. We have arbitrarily decided that this publisher allocates 15% of its overall budget to marketing, and that this percentage is spread evenly across the books the publisher has in print.

Overhead. Every publisher must also assign a certain amount of the money taken in to pay the daily expenses of running the business, many of which were mentioned above. Conse-quently, this figure could be different for different publishers. For example, a Canadian publisher need not worry about em-ployee health insurance; a New York publisher might have higher rent payments than one in the Midwest; a university press with a trade book program must pay for its sales repre-sentatives. These costs are allocated across all of the books published in a particular year, over the total number of books in print, or by using some other formula. In this case we allocate 25% of sales of each book in print to general overhead.

In short, using this model, the publisher will have made only about $1,000 profit in publishing your book on the Amish. While your colleagues might complain at the $45 cost, the publisher will complain equally loudly that your royal-ties are higher than its profits. Its profit of less than 5% of net sales is probably poorer than the publisher could have realized by investing the same money in the bank for the 5 years it took to write, produce, and sell your book.

This particular economic model is not used by any publisher we know, for any publisher who based its success on your book on the Amish would have gone bankrupt long ago. But it does point up the difficulty of being successful in scholarly publishing, and it might help you understand why a publisher could respond to your well-conceived proposal with a crass "We don't think we can sell enough copies to make the book viable."

More positively, if you understand some of the basics of publishing economics, you can make an informed decision about whether to write a book—and how to write a book a publisher will want to publish. Obviously, scholarly books *do* get published and are successful for both the author and the publisher. As we will show in subsequent chapters, this is most often the result of a mutual understanding and partnership between author and publisher.

Summary

Publishing is a business, and as an author you have to demonstrate to that business that you—and your book—are a sound investment. There are a few important questions any publisher asks before agreeing to publish a book: "Will this book add to my company's prestige? And will it add to my company's profits? Is this something the press knows how to produce and sell effectively?"

If the answer is "no" to any of these three, the publisher is not likely to accept the book. Part of the purpose of this volume is to show you how to convince the publisher that the answer to all three questions is "yes." To do so, you need to make sure that your idea is really right for a book and that you pick the right publisher for this idea. These are what we turn to in the next two chapters.

2 | So You Want to Write a Book

To have made it to where you are, you have done a lot of writing—countless papers in undergraduate and graduate school, a thesis, a dissertation, and probably journal articles. So you know quite a bit about writing. Much of this writing, however, was for a very narrow audience: your professor, fellow students, your dissertation committee, and the targeted audience of a specific journal. Likewise, each paper was probably on a narrow subject: the geology of a small Southern Californian valley, burnout among a group of New York social workers, the effects of a pet program on a group of nursing home residents. Even journal articles are usually on restricted topics: summarizing a small research project, describing a new instrument, reporting a case study, or analyzing the form of a poem.

Now, however, you want (and, in all likelihood, are expected) to write a book. Where do you start? To begin with, ask yourself what kind of book you want to write. As an academic, your obvious choices are usually a research monograph (although it is harder and harder to find a publisher for the traditional focused study type of book); a supplementary textbook, which is often a research study that draws on other studies; or a basic textbook, which is usually a synthesis of current research, organized and written so it can be taught to and easily understood by undergraduates.

It is important to be clear about this point. Each of these types of book addresses a different primary audience and serves a different purpose. Don't fall into the trap of thinking you can serve many masters equally well. You need to decide specifically what kind of book you are interested in writing— and are most qualified to write. Once you have made this decision, you need to refine your topic.

Focusing on the Right Topic

As emphasized in Chapter 1, publishing is, first and foremost, a business. As such, a publisher's ultimate questions will always be "Is there an audience for this work?" and "Can I make money on this idea?"

Consequently, before you decide that your idea warrants a book, you need to ask yourself hard questions about the commercial viability of your topic. Will interest in this topic go beyond the few specialists interested in your research? What general message do you have to offer a broader audience? And who specifically is that audience? The answers to these questions are important criteria for any publisher, who needs to determine if the press will be able to make a profit on the proposed volume.

The Essence of a Book

What makes an idea a book? There is no easy answer to this question. Certainly length is not the entire answer. We have rejected 350-page manuscripts because they were really journal articles that didn't know when to stop. Conversely (and less often), we have come across journal articles that have the potential to be expanded into a book.

This much we can say: A book must have an original perspective, a fresh approach or viewpoint. It must add significantly to the knowledge of the field. It must have a logical development, and a unique argument presented in an engaging way. And it must have an audience.

We will be discussing the audience in the next two chapters, but suffice it to say that the audience must be large enough to warrant the production and promotion investments the publisher will be making, which means that the topic must be sufficiently broad to attract enough potential buyers to repay the publisher's investment.

Not every study warrants a book; not every idea finds a publisher. Many descriptive ethnographies, evaluation studies, theoretical treatises, and textbook drafts still languish in bottom drawers of file cabinets because this issue was never addressed. The question of selecting a topic is neither insignificant nor as straightforward as it sounds.

Why, for example, does someone think it makes sense to spend countless hours studying and then writing hundreds of pages on a topic such as "McGyver and the Male Mystique"? A discussion of this topic could fit well into a book on male images in television, or be a perfectly acceptable journal article, but unless the author can document that McGyver is the most significant and influential television show today, the topic is not likely to make it into print as a book. Probably all that needs to be said on the subject can be said in the first few pages, with subsequent examples merely repeating the same points. A book on male images in television, however, has more possibilities. If it conveys something new in an interesting way, it would have some value to a relatively broad group of scholars and could be used as a supplementary text in courses on gender and the media.

When an editor recently sat on a publishing panel at an academic conference, she was asked to give the kind of advice that scholars might not want to hear but authors need to know. "Forget everything you ever learned in graduate school," she said. "We do not want narrow studies full of academic jargon.

What we are looking for are broad-based studies written in accessible language." She illustrated ways in which a broader book could be written around a narrow study. For instance, she explained how an anthropologist's in-depth research on an aboriginal menarche ritual could be used in conjunction with other studies to compare this rite of passage cross-culturally. The book could draw broad implications or arrive at a strong theoretical position about the passage from childhood to womanhood. This is a typical example of a highly specialized subject that could be reframed and turned into a book, both with an audience among researchers and with adoption potential as a supplementary text. Similarly, a group of studies on chronic illness might result in a conceptual model of the experience, both with an audience among healthcare professionals and researchers and as a supplementary text in a course on chronic illness for nurses or medical sociology students.

In sum, in contemplating writing a book, you need to take a step back from your idea and ask yourself whether your topic has a substantial audience as it stands, or whether it needs to be reframed to appeal to a publisher. With this thought in mind, let's look at two specific types of books often considered by junior scholars for their first book: the dissertation and the edited book.

The Dissertation

Rather than taking time to answer questions of applicability and marketability, many young scholars immediately send off their dissertations to the nearest publisher. Unfortunately, this is quite likely to get one of those "Dear John" letters. First, as pointed out above, you wrote your dissertation for a very small audience, your dissertation committee. Each member probably insisted certain features be incorporated into your final draft (and pity you, if the demands of two committee members conflicted). In addition, the primary purpose of the dissertation was to demonstrate your research ability, with a secondary purpose of demonstrating your writing ability. Because of the time and economic constraints, your research, and therefore your dissertation, probably had a narrow focus.

To make matters worse, the dissertation writing style is generally inappropriate for a commercial book—even a scholarly one. It tends to be repetitious, excessively documented (to prove you read everything ever published on the subject), and stilted. The needs served by a dissertation style are emphatically not the needs of the readers of a book. In fact, more than one scholar has pronounced that the dissertation finally squashes any writing ability left in an academic.

A generation ago scholarly publishers were willing to publish dissertations, but it is much less common today because of the increasingly narrow topics, the excessive jargon, and the shrinking market for this kind of book. In our experience, few dissertations today get published without extensive revision, no matter what your favorite professor says.

So the next question revolves around whether the dissertation is worth revising. Is there indeed a book buried in there somewhere? We suggest that you put it away for 6 months, then reread it when you have regained a bit more objectivity. At this stage you might well realize that you are deadly tired of the whole thing, or apathetic, or you may have moved on to something else. By all means, don't pursue the project if this is the case; you'll find yourself dreading working on the book and, in all probability, will never finish it. Just recognize it for what it did for you—got you your degree—and go on to other things.

If you are still enthusiastic, ask yourself what the document has to say that we don't already know. Upon rereading it, you might realize that there is nothing really significant or new and fresh in it. On the other hand, some real gems might be buried in all the jargon. This raises the next question in your evaluation: How much needs to be said on that subject?

You might decide that the instrument you refined has real potential, or the technical innovation you developed could be used in other settings. But such topics are more appropriate for a journal article than a book. For example, you might wish to write an article on your methodology or describe your research, pointing out that even though the sample size is small, the results warrant further investigation. Similarly, it could be the basis for a chapter in an edited book. An examination of the Billie Jean King versus Bobby Riggs tennis match might not warrant a full monograph, but it would make an important chapter in a volume on sports in twentieth-century America from a feminist perspective.

Whether you decide that you have one or two journal articles or an entire book embedded in your dissertation, be prepared to revise it extensively. We cannot emphasize this enough. You'll have to revamp your work to communicate with a broader audience, and for a different purpose than was served by your dissertation. You'll need to eliminate needless jargon, employ a livelier writing style, change passive verbs to active ones, limit the number of quotations, and delete much of the referencing to previous scholarship not specific to your theme.

You must also decide whether it is in your best interest to spend the time turning your dissertation into a book. If your department is interested in your publishing refereed articles, then writing a book will take time away from your work toward getting tenure. You might get your revised dissertation published, but at the price of losing your job.[1]

The Edited Book

If you don't want to take the time to write a whole book, should you perhaps edit one instead? If you are one of those people who has lots of ideas but trouble executing them, maybe you *should* work on an edited volume. But don't make the mistake of thinking this will be easier than writing an entire book. You will spend less time writing, but you will probably spend an equivalent amount of time directing, cajoling, organizing, chasing, and even editing the contributors' chapters.

Let's look at two types of edited books. *Reader* is the term generally used for a volume compiling previously published material. To put such a book together, you must have a clear idea of your purpose and audience (see Chapter 3), determine what topics are to be covered, and decide whether the articles reveal one consistent viewpoint or illustrate conflicting opinions. Such readers are usually developed for pedagogical rather than scholarly purposes, so you generally design them for specific courses and choose the articles accordingly. For example, an edited book for a course on women and literature in the twentieth century might include short stories, essays, poems, and even parts of a novel by such authors as Alice Walker, Maya Angelou, Joan Didion, and Eudora Welty.

Unfortunately, this kind of product is not very common anymore for any but introductory courses. Professors can put together do-it-yourself readers in the local copy shop. For such a book to find a publisher—and a buyer—you will need to differentiate it from other anthologies and provide features that a course pack would not have. For example, you would have to write scintillating introductory and concluding material as well as section introductions to link the chapters together.

A second major problem will be obtaining and paying for the requisite permissions. The copyright holders of the articles you choose might have reasons for not allowing you to use a specific article or essay, or might demand a hefty permission fee. For this reason, readers are costly for publishers to do and, therefore, require high sales expectations.

Another type of edited book incorporates original commissioned chapters. In our experience, the best edited books are conceived before a single word is written and are tightly coordinated and focused by the editor. If you have been involved in edited books, you know that they are not easy. In fact, in some ways they are much more difficult than an authored book. Securing top contributors and getting them to submit their chapters on time can be demanding and time-consuming. You must deal with a variety of egos, cross-country

Table 2.1 Characteristics of a Good Edited Book

---

1. It must be on a topic where no one person controls enough knowledge to synthesize all of the work in an area. Each contributor provides a piece of the puzzle that no individual author could synthesize.
2. It must be just as carefully designed by the editor as an authored book, with chapters flowing logically one from the other. Start with an outline as if you were writing it yourself.
3. It must be on a topic where the presentation of different perspectives or points of view is paramount.
4. The authors must all address the same set of issues, preferably following a common outline.
5. Chapters should be similar in tone, vocabulary, level of comprehension, and method of coverage.

---

or cross-national mail, missed deadlines, and poor quality chapters. No matter how efficient you are, you could end up facing the most common dilemma confronting book editors: What do you do with one or two late chapters? Do you wait and penalize the authors who produced their chapters on time, try to find a substitute author at the last minute, or drop the missing chapter and try to cover its content as best you can in the introduction? You often have to deal with contributors who don't write well, or who refuse to follow your instructions concerning revisions.

Moreover, many edited books do not hold together well as a unit. Loosely strung together articles that happen to be on a similar topic, or a collection of papers from a panel at a conference, do not generally make a good book. They can form the basis of a good book, but require a lot of work on everyone's behalf to create a tight focus. Chapters need a lot of input from the editor—making sure the theme emerges logically and is carried through in all the chapters, editing for style so they flow together, and eliminating redundancies.

What constitutes a good edited book? Some of the elements are listed in Table 2.1. Even then, authored books generally sell better to individuals and libraries and are usually preferred as supplementary texts. In addition, if you are the author, rather than the editor, you can ensure that the book covers the topic in a manner that best reflects your beliefs and viewpoint. Perhaps equally important, an authored book could count toward tenure; an edited book seldom does.

Getting Down to Writing

Ah, yes. There's the rub. Once you have decided upon a topic appropriate for a book, you have to get down to the actual process of writing. Books on how to write are plentiful, even ones with specific writing exercises.[2] And books such as Strunk and White's *The Elements of Style* will help you overcome your "dissertation death" technique. What you need to remember is the difference between being a *writer* and being an *editor*.

Often, when people first sit down to write, they begin a sentence and immediately take a dislike to the way it is worded and start again. This is the editor interfering with the writer. Both are essential, but both should be kept in their places. The writer writes, the editor edits. The writer writes without worrying about what the niggly editorial commentary is saying— "Oh, what would so and so say about that?" or "I don't think that is the proper way to say it," or "Is that the correct academic style?" The writer just writes without stopping to rethink, to correct, to stand back and pass judgment. Simply write on your subject. If it is one that requires research, you should still know your subject well enough by the time you sit down to write, and you can go back and fill in the details such as place, date, and exact statistics later.

The editor is as important as the writer but functions very differently. Once you have written a rough draft, preferably after a day or a week, go back and look at your writing with the critical, objective eye of the editor. The editor is supposed to question: Does this make sense? Is this section necessary? Could this point be put more succinctly? The editor will help you get rid of the parts that are important to you but no one else. Cutting is the best editorial tool of all. Write the first draft without worrying about the length, but then be willing to cut drastically to get to the core of your subject.

You might notice that we just mentioned "first draft." This is an important concept and one that will lead you to second, third, even more drafts, however many it takes to get it right. So, write without editing, then edit, then rewrite without editing, then edit once again. When you exhaust your own critical eye as an editor, enlist the assistance of your spouse, your colleagues, your students, your trusted friends . . . and ask them to be brutal. It is hard work and it is tough on the ego, but the final product, whether book, chapter, or article, will be better because of this process.

Before and during the writing process, think about your reader and about getting your message out to the widest possible audience. Some scholars seem to want to write only to their own inner circle, in language that nobody but the chosen few can understand, on topics that few others would care to know about. Instead, write as if you had to explain everything, from the beginning of the theoretical premise to the full explanation for the rationale behind your research method. You owe the reader an explanation of the relevance to your work of any references you make or examples you use or works you cite. Fix an ideal reader in your mind—a bright student in one of your classes, a junior colleague to whom you wish to explain your ideas, your dean—and write with that person in your mind's eye.

Summary

At the end of the publishing panel our editor sat on last year, some people came up to ask her questions that they hadn't wanted to air in the public forum.

"What do you think about a book on irrigation systems in Nigeria?" an earnest young man asked. She couldn't believe that all her strongly stated points had not gotten through to him.

"Well, maybe you could expand it into a book on the ecology of Nigeria, the colonial legacy, and so on," she began. His eyes clouded over; all he wanted to do was write up that study. "On the other hand," she added, "maybe you should just write a journal article."

We don't know what he did, but we do know what most publishers would do if he wrote a book on Nigerian irrigation systems. They would send a letter, "Dear Dr. Waters: Thank you for your interest in Ponds Publishers. Unfortunately, our market research leads us to believe that we would be unable to sell enough copies to recoup our production and promotion investments." Certainly, no one wants to hear that. So choose your topic wisely and spend time deciding how you can make it appropriate for the widest possible audience. Once you have accomplished that, you're ready to start looking for a publisher.

Notes

1. For a fuller discussion, we recommend another book in this series, *Getting Tenure,* by Marcia Lynn Whicker, Jennie Jacobs Kronenfeld, and Ruth Ann Strickland.

2. See Additional Resources section for some books designed to help your writing.

3 | Finding the Right Publisher

You will undoubtedly spend months or years working on your book. You might first spend years in the field, the archive, the computer room, the library. You'll then devote substantial time to puzzling out your data and writing multiple drafts of the manuscript. Yet how often does this diligent tale of hard work end badly because the wrong publisher is selected? You've all heard these "tales of the field" from your colleagues:

- They never promoted my book to anthropologists. Not surprisingly, it sold only 24 copies.
- It took 4 years to come out, and even then they printed the map upside down.
- There were so many typographical errors in it that I was embarrassed to show it to the colleagues for whom I wrote it.
- They made me rewrite it for an audience of congenital idiots.
- It was never reviewed.

These horror stories are all too common and serve to reinforce the traditional ambivalence scholars have toward pub-

AUTHOR'S NOTE: This is a revised version of an article appearing in *Cultural Anthropology Methods Newsletter*, February 1992. Reprinted by permission of the publisher.

lishers. But many of these tales of woe could have been avoided if the author had invested a fraction of the time spent on writing in researching publishers for the book. Along with endless complaints about publishers (many of them justified), we hear stories about the author who published with Plagiarist Press or Mediocre Monographs for reasons such as: "Their sales rep came by just as I finished the manuscript," "I got stuck in a broken elevator with the editor at a conference," or "They asked me."

Done right, researching publishers enables you to publish your book in a fashion that meets your goals, hopes, and expectations for your carefully crafted work. But doing it right requires an investment of time and energy in learning a bit about the world of publishing. In this way, finding the right publisher is not unlike the process of conducting research—choosing a topic, designing a research strategy, doing your library homework, going out into the field, then drawing proper conclusions.

Picking a Topic

In Chapter 2 we discussed how to decide whether your topic is worth a book. Choosing your topic and the audience to which you are gearing that topic are primary issues that you must address before you can pick an appropriate publisher. As we discussed in Chapter 1, different publishers occupy different niches in the marketplace. Your book topic might be shaped in a variety of ways, depending on whether a scholarly, reference, text, or serious nonfiction publisher is handling the book. One publisher will want you to simplify the level of writing and add class exercises and discussion questions to better sell it as a textbook. Another might urge you to eliminate your data presentations in favor of a more detailed description of your theory, hoping to sell it as an important theoretical work for professionals in your field. Each of these niches has its own economic demands. No publisher will handle your book if it feels that the niche you have chosen for your work is smaller than its sales needs.

So try to identify a niche for your book and find a publisher who publishes for that niche. A book on the culture of a distinct geographical area in the United States might find a home with a university press that specializes in regional books. Generally, however, whichever niche you ultimately choose, use the maxim "broader is better" in trying to fill it. If your book is for graduate students and professionals in social work, then try to address as broad a group of them as possible. If you are targeting the junior-level course in Renaissance literature, make sure your book idea completely fills that niche. Doing so will make your proposal as attractive as possible to the publishers you approach.

Although some niches might ultimately be too small for most publishers, few topic areas are so narrow and unconnected to other topics that, if you are willing to negotiate the parameters of the topic, a book on that subject is unpublishable. For example, you might collect 20 rejection letters for your study of marital violence in a small village in Costa Rica. On the other hand, similar to the research on an aboriginal menarche ritual mentioned in Chapter 2, if your data can become a small part of a large comparative study of marital violence patterns in Latin America, or if the case material can support a theoretical work on the connection between machismo and marital violence, or even be the springboard for a textbook on cross-cultural marital violence, it is more likely that someone will publish one of the broader book ideas.

Designing a Research Strategy

With your topic in hand, the next step is to design your research strategy. As with any research project, a clear understanding of your goals is essential to designing your project: in this case, picking the right publisher. Your goals might be different from those of your colleagues, so you need to decide what is most important to you as you look for a publisher. You need to ask yourself why exactly you want to write this book and what specifically you want out of it. Depending upon how you answer these questions, you might wish to look for any of the following in a publisher:

- Money. Who will pay the largest amount in royalties and/or advances?
- Aesthetics. Whose book will be the most attractive looking?
- Prestige. Which publishing house will be most favorably regarded for tenure or promotion decisions?
- Advertising and distribution. Which press will most aggressively sell the book to your colleagues? Who will be best able to market it overseas?
- Pricing. Who will price it in such a way that your colleagues or their students can best afford to buy it? Who will publish it in hardcover only, paper only, or dual editions?
- Speed of publication. Who will have your book in the hands of readers the quickest?
- Specific markets. If there are specific groups of people for whom you are writing, which press best reaches those groups?

No one publisher does *all* of those things better than other publishers. So it is worthwhile to rank these elements, and other considerations you have, in order of importance, then focus on publishers who meet your most important criteria. For example, one publisher might produce beautiful hardcover, dust-jacketed volumes, but take 18 months in production. If you know someone else is working on a similar book, or if your data is time sensitive, then that publisher would be an inappropriate choice. Similarly, if you know your book has high potential as a supplementary text, you might wish to consider a publisher who will put out a paperback edition simultaneously with the hardcover. You must decide which goals are more important to you.

Identifying your goals might also help you shape your topic, because certain goals fit better with certain types of publishers. If the key goal of your publishing a book is to help you get tenure, then you might look toward a university press and design your topic around their interests. If, on the other hand, you're hoping for a large advance to buy that cabin in Maine you've always wanted, then you should think more about writing a textbook and conceptualize your writing project accordingly.

Do You Need an Agent?

At this point you may be wondering if you should approach an agent. After all, you might reason, finding the right publisher is what they do. Generally speaking, however, agents are seldom warranted for a scholarly author. Moreover, few agents are willing to take on an unproven author. They usually want evidence of past accomplishments and future potential, because the money they make is a percentage of whatever you, the author, makes. It does not pay for them to spend the time necessary to place your project unless sales potential is high. Unfortunately, few scholarly books fit this bill, as the model in Chapter 1 shows.

On the other hand, more and more scholars are writing books for the "serious" trade market. Deborah Tannen made the crossover with *You Just Don't Understand*, and Albert Haurani did it with *A History of the Arab Peoples*. Both had something meaningful to say, a distinctive point of view, and an accessible style. An agent would be useful here, but again might be unwilling to take on an unproven author.

Generally speaking, if you can interest an agent, you are probably working on a trade book. If your interest is in writing a scholarly book, you can probably find a publisher yourself. If you would still like to find an agent, check *Publisher's Weekly*, the *Literary Market Place*, the Society of Author Representatives (SAR), or the Independent Literary Agents Association. (See Additional Resources for the addresses of these organizations.)

Doing Your Homework

Just as you will do a literature search before entering the field, gathering information on potential publishers from available sources is a crucial preliminary step in finding the right publisher.

First, build your bibliography. In this case, look on your bookshelf to see whose books regularly appear there. In all likelihood, those presses have an interest in your subject. Examine the dates on these books to make sure their publishers are consistently publishing in the area. Similarly, check your mailbox. Keep flyers you receive from various publishers over a period of time. Investigate who regularly advertises in conference programs or journals in your discipline. If you and your colleagues are not on a publisher's mailing list and are not included as part of its advertising budget, that press is less likely to reach your audience effectively than a publisher who regularly advertises to you and people like yourself. You can also check the exhibits at your academic meetings. What publishers attend, and what kinds of books do they display? At the same time, you can contact the editors or marketing personnel at conventions. Take advantage of their presence to discuss their house's potential interest.

Similarly, sales representatives who visit your campus are good sources of information. Rather than dreading their visit, view it as a possible learning experience. Ask them what sells and what doesn't, what their publishers are interested in, and how those publishers market their product. Many sales representatives are aspiring editors eager to sponsor new authors for their company. The experience can thus be mutually beneficial.

Next, use the library. One volume that should be consulted is *Literary Market Place* (LMP), published annually by R. R. Bowker. LMP is the phone directory of the book publishing industry and contains names and addresses of presses, their subject areas of publication, the number of titles they published last year, and the total number of titles they have in print. In addition, it often includes the names of appropriate acquisitions editors. The American Association of University Presses (AAUP) also publishes an annual directory that provides similar information on university presses.

Finally, start networking and interviewing informants. Many of your colleagues have had dealings with publishers and have information that could be of value. Because scholars tend to have only anecdotal information about publishing and publishers, their information might not always be reliable. A colleague might have had an unsatisfactory experience for a variety of reasons, none currently valid. Even anecdotal data is better than none, however, and these people might be able to provide you with contacts within the network of acquisitions editors who will decide whether to publish your book.

Go Into the Field

By now you should be ready to enter the field in your publisher search. You have selected a niche and a topic appropriate for that niche. You have developed a list of potential publishers who work in your area. You have narrowed that list to the most likely houses, using information garnered from your colleagues, from LMP, and from your own observations on how they advertise and what they've published in the past.

If your network has provided you with an informant inside a publishing house, use it. If not, you might have to enter the publishing world without a ready-made informant in place. In either case, your background research is never a substitute for direct work in the field. So contact publishers on your short list and get some firsthand data.

The person with whom you wish to speak is, most often, the acquisitions editor (sometimes called the acquiring, or sponsoring, editor) for your discipline. Your research should have turned up this person's name, phone number, and bizarre behavioral habits (after a number of years in the publishing business, most have them). The acquisitions editor is the gatekeeper in most publishing houses, the person who recommends publication of your book to the press's publications board; who has to answer to the house for its success or failure; who shepherds it through the development and production process; and who champions the project among jaded marketing directors, color-blind cover designers, and everyone else involved with the project. The editor is also likely to be your best source of information about the press. Depending on your preferred style of interaction, you can reach the editor by phone or face-to-face at national conferences, which most editors regularly attend. Editors also regularly visit many university campuses, so can occasionally be encountered on your home turf. Or, if the publishing house is close, try to set up a meeting at the editor's office.

As with most interviewing, questions will emerge from the discussion. But there are some structured starting points:

- What are the strengths of the press?
- What are its customary procedures and timetable for reviewing submitted proposals or manuscripts?
- How long should a manuscript be?
- What are the standard terms of a contract?
- What are the standard practices and timetable for producing a book?
- How do they price and market books? What audiences do they reach and how do they reach them?
- What is the nature and focus of their list in your field?
- After you describe your project, can the editor tell you how likely the press is to be interested in your book? What would make it more appealing?
- What information do they need to make a publications decision?

If you are a skillful interviewer, you can often induce the editor to compare his or her press with others on your list, or elicit the names of the editor's counterparts at other presses (and their bizarre behavioral habits). The editor might also get involved in shaping your project to specifically fit the press's needs, making his or her sponsorship, and therefore publication, more likely.

With a series of interviews and reinterviews, and careful analysis of the results, you are now ready to submit your prospectus or manuscript to the presses whose interests seem most consonant with your goals. Getting to know the editor might influence this decision; often a good working relationship with an editor who is enthusiastic about your project can result in a better book and an enjoyable writing experience.

You will note that we mentioned presses in the plural. We recommend that you always try more than one. When you submit an article to a journal, that journal usually expects that you will not submit the same article to other journals at the same time. This is seldom the case in book publishing. You may submit your proposal simultaneously to as many publishers as you wish, although it is courteous to inform the publishers that this is a multiple submission.

A query letter is generally unnecessary if you have already spoken to the editor. If you have not yet been in contact, a telephone call to the editor, describing the project and your qualifications and asking if he or she would be interested in the book you are planning, will get you more information than a query letter. Every editor is willing to take a few minutes to listen to your description, ask enough questions to decide if it is something of interest to the publisher, and probably recommend another press if it is inappropriate. When you are ready to submit your proposal, you can remind the editor of the telephone call and thus get your manuscript off the slush pile, the killing field of any publishing house.

How important is it to getting published to have contact with an editor? A study done in the 1970s by Walter Powell, a sociologist at University of Arizona, demonstrated that, while manuscripts submitted over the transom (i.e., those that come unsolicited through the mail) to a scholarly press had a 0.5% chance of being accepted for publication; those odds increased to 8% for someone who had some prior contact with the press, and 35% when directly solicited by the editor (Powell, 1985, p. 169). Our own experience confirms these statistics.

Summary

Finding the right publisher means you must spend some time conducting research. The final choices will reflect what you discovered and also your own goals and objectives. And remember, there is never just one "right publisher."

In the next chapter, we will translate your publishing knowledge and your budding relationship with an acquisitions editor into a book proposal that he or she couldn't possibly turn down. It's time to write a prospectus.

4 | Preparing a Book Prospectus

To sell your book idea to a publisher, you need three things: a hook, a line, and a buyer. Most of the thousands of proposals submitted to publishers each year receive scant attention from overworked and harried acquisitions editors. Thus your proposal needs to grab an editor's attention quickly (the hook), preferably in the first paragraph of a cover letter that accompanies the book prospectus. Use an imaginative metaphor, an irresistible mystery, a good title, or link your book to a hot topic or recent best-seller. In one recent cover letter to a proposal on caregivers, the author included a brief transcription of an interview with a grandmother, explaining how looking after her grandchild had changed her life and describing the resulting worries and hardships and the accompanying joy. The excerpt was enough to make the editor want to know more. Another cover letter might link a book on the need for educational reform to the latest political rhetoric.

Tell the editor up front what the book is about (the line), not after several introductory pages of text. He or she might never read that far. A Broadway producer, when approached by hopeful screenwriters, used to have them write their idea

AUTHOR'S NOTE: This chapter is a revised version of an article appearing in *Cultural Anthropology Methods Newsletter*, October 1992. Reprinted by permission of the publisher.

on the back of his business card; he felt that if the author had a good, clear idea, the card was more than adequate in size. Others suggest that you pretend to be in a room full of the ideal audience for buying your book, and you have 30 seconds to tell them about it. Because your book will probably be sold through a paragraph-long piece of advertising copy, or a 30-second pitch by a sales representative this exercise is not an abstract one. If you cannot condense your book description to a paragraph, you probably need to conceptualize it better.

Finally, briefly identify who you are trying to reach with your book (the buyer, or audience) so the editor can easily determine if your book is appropriate for the house's list.

With the editor hooked, you now have the luxury of presenting your book prospectus in greater detail. The prospectus explains your plans and goals in writing a book. More than a simple outline of the book's contents, it should give the publisher sufficient information to come to an informed publication decision, based on the book's intellectual contribution, market potential, and production complexities. Publishers receive many book proposals each week, so care in developing the book prospectus should improve your chances of getting published. Lavish as much care and thought on it as you would on a major grant proposal.

The process of preparing a book prospectus is often helpful to you as well as the publisher. It forces you to focus your thoughts about the project, to define the organization of the book, to make decisions on crucial issues like length, timetable, level of writing, and audience that otherwise might not be addressed until you are mired in the project.

You can structure a book prospectus in many different ways. A few publishers have specific formats to follow, so ask before you start. In almost all cases, however, publishers are looking for the following kinds of information:

1. Intellectual Contribution

Here is where you demonstrate to the publisher (and to those who may review the book for the publisher) the nature and importance of the book's contribution. *Briefly* (one to three pages) describe the subject matter of the book and its importance to the field. You will want to comment on your methodological and theoretical approach, the level of complexity of the ideas and the writing, and the topics you plan to cover. Is it a "broad brush" approach, or a detailed comprehensive treatment of the topic? Will the book be applied, a report on current research, or a review of the literature?

Expect that the initial reader of the prospectus—the acquisitions editor—is not fully versed on the importance of your ideas, findings, and contribution to the intellectual debate, and is probably unfamiliar with all of the specialized jargon of your subfield. Conversely, the publisher might send this description to one of your colleagues to review, so the description needs to convey, in jargon-free terms, that you are an expert in this area and capable of writing a good book on this topic. Keep in mind the questions the editor will be asking: Is the topic timely? Will it be timely a year after it is written, when the published book comes off the presses? Is it cutting-edge material and, if so, how far in the future will that edge be? Does it have a fresh, wide appeal? Is it significant? Are the facts accurate, the research and references up to date? Be specific in explaining your rationale for writing the book and how it fills a need that you have identified.

2. The Audience

This part of the prospectus is usually the hardest one for the scholar to write, yet it is given the most scrutiny by the publisher. You need to know for whom you are writing the book and be able convey that information to the publisher in the most detailed manner possible. Only that information allows the publisher to make a calculated guess as to the size of the market.

What kind of information is the publisher looking for? The average professor's answer, "This book will be of use to psychologists, their graduate and undergraduate students, other social scientists, and the informed public," is absolutely useless to publishers. It is a rare book that can appeal to such a broad range of readers. Before you question why, think carefully about the different needs, interests, and academic preparations of these diverse audiences. Such statements leave the editor wondering which audience would really find it appealing and if that audience is one the press can reach. What *is* useful to the editor is specific information and specialized knowledge that you have but the publisher might not. In drafting this section, think about the following questions:

General Audience. What field(s) or discipline(s) will be core audiences for the book? Which subfields within those broad subjects will this book address most directly? For example, within psychology, who would be most interested in your book—humanistic, developmental, or family psychologists? Are there other, secondary audiences for the book? Would psychiatric mental health nurses find it useful?

Level. Is the book to be written at a level appropriate for your colleagues? Graduate students? Advanced undergraduates? Lower-division students or nonmajors? Nonacademic professionals? The general public? As mentioned above, it is an exceptional book that can be successfully written for and marketed to all of those audiences.

Lists. As we pointed out in previous chapters, most scholarly publishers sell their books through direct mail solicitation to interested groups of professionals. Where will the publisher find lists of people to whom it can promote the book? These can include divisions or interest groups in a major academic society, specialized research networks, conference participation lists, subscribers to journals, magazines, or newsletters in your area, personal mailing lists. If you know the approximate size of the list(s) and/or the name of a contact, be sure to provide this information.

Courses. If you believe your book will be useful for university instruction, provide some supporting data. In which courses, at what level, and at what kind of university would this book be used? As a main text or supplemental text? At approximately how many universities around the country are these courses taught? How often? Are they required or elective? How many students do they typically enroll? Are class sizes increasing or decreasing? If you teach such a course yourself, provide information from your own experience. Try also to provide the names and affiliation of others who teach this course. Sometimes your professional organizations will have some of this information.

Specialized Sales. Are there special groups to which the publisher might be able to sell large quantities? A book on pharmacology may interest drug companies, which would distribute copies to physicians. An association of directors who work with volunteers might want to share with its members a book on working with older volunteers. Are there appropriate book clubs the publisher might approach, such as the History Book Club, the Astronomy Book Club, or the Behavioral Sciences Book Club? Do you have contacts overseas who might facilitate the sale of translation rights, or who might arrange distribution?

Remember, be realistic. Comparing your book to Stephen Hawking's *A Brief History of Time*, saying the same people will buy your book, is hardly likely to impress your editor. On the other hand, if you believe that it will be a core text in a course that is growing in importance in your field, point that out to the editor, supplying data showing how the offerings have increased over the past few years.

3. Competition

Your book is unique, but the person who buys your book also buys others. So the question of competition is relevant and important to the publisher attempting to assess the size of the potential audience and the competitive advantages your book affords. What other books address the same audience? What distinguishes your book from these others? What unique selling propositions does it offer? If the publisher has similar books, will yours compete directly or complement them? In textbook publishing, you are expected to list all major competing books for the course and comment on your proposed book in relation to them.

4. Qualifications of the Author

What experience, background, or other qualifications do you bring to the project that uniquely qualify you to undertake it? The editor will be looking both at your area of expertise and at your previous writing experience. Do you plan on using a consultant for chapters in which you might not be fully qualified? Answer these questions in a paragraph and attach a current *vita*. If the book has numerous contributors, include their current affiliations and a very brief description of their qualifications.

5. Technical Specifications of the Book

The publisher also will want to know some practical details in order to estimate publication costs and schedule:

- How long will the book be (in double-spaced manuscript pages)?
- What is your schedule for completing a first draft? A final version? What is already available for the publisher to review?
- Are there tables, figures, maps, photographs, or other nontext material to be included? Approximately how many of each?

Might any of this material pose special production problems for the publisher?

- Are there other technical problems of which the publisher should be aware? For example, figures that won't reduce to the publisher's standard page size, permissions needed to reprint copyrighted material, restrictions placed upon you by granting agencies, or your own nonnegotiable contract demands.
- Is the manuscript available on computer disk? If so, specify the format, software, and system.
- If you have any suggestions for either informed but impartial reviewers or people who shouldn't review the manuscript for one reason or another, make those suggestions.

6. *The Outline and Writing Samples*

Next you need to explain in greater detail the specific organization of the book. This part of the prospectus can be prepared either as an outline or in the form of chapter abstracts. Let the editor see how your ideas flow into one another. Give a rationale for why topic A precedes topic B. This material will be given the closest scrutiny by the publisher's reviewers. It is often helpful to attach either a sample chapter or one of your published articles on the topic to demonstrate your writing style.

Final Reminders

Most publishers receive many book proposals each week, so the more care you take, the better your chances of getting beyond the first glance through. Use active words, such as argue, analyze, examine, illustrate, illuminate. Ask yourself how much information *you* would need to get engaged and to understand the book, and make sure you supply it. Then have a colleague who knows your work look over the final product and make any suggestions to improve clarity. Finally, give it one last proofreading for grammar, spelling, and sexist language.

The function of this document is to sell a specific press on your idea. Tailor your proposal to the interests of the editor who will make the decision, and the reviewers who are likely to examine it for the editor. Having already spoken to that editor to ascertain his or her interests (see Chapter 3), you should have some idea of how to present the ideas. If you are submitting to several presses, feel free to vary the proposals to each one, highlighting what you think would interest that press. If you are unclear on how to present your proposal, call the editor again for guidance. This will also remind the editor that the proposal is coming, which might give your proposal more attention than the others that come in that day's mail.

We have included a sample prospectus and the accompanying cover letter in the Appendix.

Summary

Editorial decision making is not a science. The publisher's decision is based on a variety of factors, many of which have little to do with the quality of either the ideas or the writing. The manner in which you present your proposal can make an enormous difference in whether you are offered a publishing contract. Try to grab the editor's attention immediately and follow with a brief description of the subject and the audience.

Then develop a sound prospectus that clearly explains what the book is about, who is interested in it, why you are qualified to write it, and what technical problems it might entail. Editors appreciate this professionalism—it is a sign of an author who can deliver a good book. But it still has to get over the next hurdle, the review process. We turn to that next.

5 | The Review Process

Let's assume that your proposal is now on the editor's desk. You called the editor before sending your materials, and in your cover letter you reminded her (let's assume this editor is a woman) of that call and her response. You have a great hook in the letter, which perks her interest immediately. At this point your proposal has survived the first hurdle, getting an overburdened, beleaguered editor to read your proposal carefully. Because you followed our suggestions, the proposal is outstanding, enumerating explicitly the rationale for your book, its intended audience, its specifications, and the outline.

And suddenly the overworked, harassed editor is more than a little interested; she's excited. Here is someone with a good idea who cares enough about his or her project to prepare a well-thought-out proposal. Remember, this editor is in publishing because she loves books, and she is probably in scholarly publishing because she wants to see scholarly work and important research shared. She *wants* to find a good book, and your proposal holds promise of that.

Your proposal has thus weathered the *in-house review*. This process may take from as little as a day up to several weeks, depending on whether the editor is working on a time-consuming project, visiting campuses, or attending conventions. At this point you will most likely receive either a letter or a telephone call from the editor or her assistant, informing you that your proposal has indeed passed the in-house review and is being sent out for peer review.

Peer Review

Editors in scholarly publishing houses are generalists and probably not expert in all aspects of your field; they rely on your peers to inform them on the importance, accuracy, and timeliness of your proposal.

Usually a publishing house and each editor will have a group of reviewers whose opinions they value. These reviewers are authorities in the field, people the editors have met and respect, and possibly authors published by the house. Good reviewers also are objective, have an open mind, and are willing to give constructive feedback.

In deciding upon what reviewers to ask, the editor will take into consideration any information you might have included in your proposal, such as avoiding someone who disagrees violently with anything you write. For example, one of us recently sent a well-written, engrossing proposal to a well-known researcher in the area. The resulting review was negative in the extreme, surprising the editor, who was disposed to favor the proposal. Upon looking into it a little further, however, she discovered that the author and the reviewer had been feuding for several years. On the other hand, you might also wish to recommend one or more colleagues whose authority you respect. Your editor might elect to use one or more of these experts.

The editor or her assistant calls the reviewers to ask if they can look at your proposal within a specified time frame, sometimes 2 weeks, sometimes 6 weeks or longer, depending upon the length and complexity of the proposal and how excited the editor is about the project. The reviewer is usually asked to respond to some standard questions and possibly

some specific questions the editor thought about when reading your proposal. Questions will concern the importance of
the subject, the coverage of the topic, any additions or changes
the reviewer believes are necessary to recommend that the
publisher offer a contract, and an assessment of the market
potential. For example, the reviewers could be asked if they
would personally purchase the book, recommend it to their
colleagues or students, or adopt it as a core or supplementary
text in appropriate courses (see Figure 5.1).

Typically, an editor will try to get two or three reviews, more
if the investment will be particularly high, or the area is a new
one for the press. It's marvelous if all the reviewers agree a
proposed book is great, wonderful, destined to be a classic.
If all condemn it for faulty logic, outdated theories, and other
terminal faults, the editor (and you) might be disappointed,
but at least you will know that investing in the project as it
stands isn't worthwhile for either of you. And as we will see
later in this chapter, you might learn something useful even
from negative feedback.

Often, however, people being people, there is disagreement
over the exact worth of the book and what kinds of changes
would improve it. The editor must then ponder what to make
of the differing reviews. As we will see in a moment, she may
enlist your help in integrating them.

All this could take a couple of weeks or 2 or 3 months,
depending upon a variety of factors, many of them outside
the editor's control. We recommend that you call at regular
intervals to ask about the status of your proposal. Following
up also gives you an opportunity to lobby the editor on the
merits of your proposal. And if your proposal is sitting there,
waiting for her or her assistant to write a rejection letter, at
least you will know to eliminate that publisher from your list.
If contacting you is several down on her list of things to do,
you will get her to respond quickly; the squeaky wheel does
get the attention. If the delay is beyond her control, at the least
she will probably make a point to contact you just as soon as
the reviews are available, and the resulting conversation might

September 10, 1993

Dr. Goode Review
Humanities Department
Writing State University
Reading, ND 54321

Dear Dr. Review:

Thank you for agreeing to review the enclosed proposal, *Getting Published* by Christine S. Smedley, Mitch Allen and Associates. We appreciate your willingness to take time from your busy schedule to give your input on this project. Could you please address the following questions:

1. Do you agree with the authors' assessment of current books on the market? Is a short book on getting published needed? Will the proposed book meet that need? What does this book propose to offer that is significantly different from other publications on the market?

2. What is your opinion of the organization and content? Is the sequence of material logical? Are there any obvious omissions? Should any chapters or topics be added? Deleted?

3. Do you agree with the authors' appraisal of the primary audiences for the book? Will the coverage appeal to those audiences? Will they find the material useful?

4. Would you buy the book for your personal library? If you were teaching a seminar on getting published, would you use this book as a text? A supplementary text?

5. The authors mention that they will include a sample proposal. What additional kinds of illustrative material would you find useful?

6. What are the main strengths of the book? The main weaknesses?

7. Do you recommend publication? Please explain why or why not.

Again, thank you for taking the time to respond to my request. I look forward to receiving your proposal by October 15. If it is more convenient, fax to my attention at the number listed above.

Cordially,

Frances Borghi
Senior Editorial Assistant

Figure 5.1. A Sample Review Letter

result in some editorial feedback that will help you in further refining your ideas.

Similarly, your input might further help your editor as she considers your proposal. For example, you might be able to give her some additional information on a small society that you recently came across whose members would be responsive to your book. Remember, you are trying to sell yourself and your proposed book to the press. Being timid about calling will not further your cause.

So we have three scenarios: (a) All reviewers rave about your proposal, including the potential sales of the book. Congratulations; chances are high that you will be receiving a contract offer very soon. (b) Reviewers might differ about the proposal, but recommend publication if the author makes certain changes. We'll tell you below what to make of such reviews. (c) All reviewers are unenthusiastic about your proposal. Don't give up yet!

If the reviewers make suggestions for improving the proposed book, the editor will contact you and probably send "blind" copies (with identification of the reviewer masked) of the reviews, asking for your response. She probably will have in mind changes that she believes essential to the success of the book, but might be willing to listen to your rationale for why other changes should or should not be made.

Read the reviews carefully and try to maintain objectivity. We know it's hard to be impartial in the face of critical feedback, even if it is designed to be constructive (which it isn't always). But everyone wants the best book possible—you as author, the editor as the one who must defend your book to the publications committee, even the reviewers who are interested in the advancement of their field.

Be amenable to making necessary changes, but also be willing to contest those suggestions that you believe damage the value and scope of the book. Remember, however, your editor will want to know *why* you maintain that you are right and the reviewer is wrong. In addition, you must be able to give a clear, well-considered rebuttal to any negative review.

When you have seriously considered all the reviewer comments, call your editor and explain what changes you are willing to make. She will undoubtedly ask you to put your plan in writing, but contacting her directly will encourage her response, and the exchange might result in a third option—a combination of the reviewer's suggestions and your own opinions.

Once you have responded, your editor must once again look over your proposal, all reviewer comments, and your response. There are three editorial axioms that come into play here:

1. Books that don't review well, don't sell well.
2. Books that review well often, but not always, sell well.
3. As an editor, if you have serious doubts, forget it, no matter what the reviewers say.

The editor's job may be relatively simple if the reviews are all negative or, at best, lukewarm. It's not that easy if the reviewers disagree. As she considers your project, she will be asking herself if it has the potential to be a *good* book—in other words, one that sells and increases rather than detracts from the publisher's reputation—and if indeed the press can effectively market it. In addition, every good editor has gut reactions at least once in a while; sometimes they are right, sometimes wrong, but an editor will always take them into account. If, for whatever reason, she wants to say "no," the reviews will need to be very compelling to get her to change her mind.

The editor will also be asking herself how deeply she feels about the project and if she is willing to go to bat for it. She will have to do just that. Managerial controls are implicit in any decision to offer a contract. Although who sits on an editorial committee varies with the publisher, your editor will have to persuade that august body that your book will be good for the company.

If the ultimate answer is "We are unable to offer to undertake publication at this time," don't give up. An editor may, if she feels they are useful, send the negative reviews to you, expressing the hope that they will help you revise your proposal; however, she is under no obligation to share the reviews with you. She may just pick out specific quotes to include in a rejection letter, or allude to the reviewers' comments. For example, she may say that the reviewers indicated that the market is too limited or that your observations are dated.

If the reviews are not enclosed, you might want to call and ask for copies, but be prepared to get a negative response. The house might not encourage sending them out. Or the editor might have not enclosed them to save your feelings.

If the rejection letter or the reviews themselves point to specific reasons why your proposal was rejected, now is the time to rethink your project. Put it and the reviews away for a couple of weeks, then look at it with fresh eyes. Ask yourself if there is any truth to the criticisms. Can you refocus the main idea; handle opposing viewpoints or contradictory research more thoughtfully; broaden the intended audience?

In Chapter 3 we mentioned the possibility of simultaneous submissions. Obviously, doing so could save you much time. You might, however, want to submit your proposal to one publisher and then the next sequentially. What you forfeit in time, you might gain by being able to reformulate the proposal, to address concerns raised by the reviews received, before sending it off to the next publisher on your list.

It is important to point out that publishers make mistakes all the time. Famous authors have tales about papering their walls with rejection slips, and publishers tell similar tales of rejecting the book that went on to sell millions of copies and launch the career of a Hemingway or a James Newman. Newman, for example, approached an editor at Harper with an idea for writing a 500-page book on mathematical thought and its development. The editor, who had an impressive record of publishing notable books, told him no one would buy such a book. But he was proven wrong. Newman's *The World of Mathematics*, evolving into a four-volume set, was picked up by Simon & Schuster. It went on to sell hundreds of thousands of sets.

Summary

The review process is designed to help the editor make an informed decision about the worth and marketability of your proposed book. The more carefully drafted your proposal is, the better your chances are of getting positive reviews. But remember not to let negative reviews overly discourage you. Stand firm for what you believe is essential for your book, but also seriously consider the recommendations the reviews make and be willing to change your focus where warranted.

Finally, keep in mind that, even with reviews, the final decision is, to some degree, subjective. The editor makes a decision, then tries to sell the project to the press's advisory board. Wrong answers are common. Lots of poor books get published, and lots of potentially exceptional books are rejected.

But not yours. Because your cover letter got the editor interested and because your strong proposal got her hooked; and because you are developing a personal relationship with your editor, you have been offered a contract. Should you sign it? Never fear. In the next chapter we will try to explain what a typical contract contains.

6 | The Publishing Contract

It's been weeks, maybe months of phone calls, faxes, proposals, drafts, revised drafts, and reviews. Finally, you and your publisher have agreed. Your book is one that the publisher wants to sell, and this publisher is one that suits your needs. Confidently, your acquisition editor tells you, "The contract is on its way."

Soon a thick envelope arrives (or sometimes, in tight situations, the omnipresent fax hums into action). It's great to know that your project has been accepted, but what sense can you make out of the clauses and conditions in the contract? What can you negotiate? What can't you negotiate? Should you call a lawyer?

It's easy to be intimidated by a lengthy legal document such as a publishing contract. After all, what it says will determine how your book will be presented and how you will be compensated. Maybe you've heard horror stories from colleagues who believe they were dealt with unfairly by a publisher and felt powerless because of the terms of their agreement. And the often obtuse language for which most contracts are notorious doesn't help relieve any potential anxiety. It is not necessary, however, to immediately run to a lawyer. "Contract anxiety" can be alleviated by understanding how and why a publisher frames its agreements. Later in this chapter we'll go over the individual components of a typical agreement.

Guidelines for Negotiating a Contract

But first, a few important points to keep in mind when approaching a written agreement:

❶ *A contract is designed to cover worst-case scenarios.* A contract is like an insurance policy for both parties. Much of what it covers doesn't represent the regular practices of a publishing enterprise. A publishing house being destroyed by fire or flood doesn't happen every day; neither does one going bankrupt or being sold (although it has been known to happen). Authors, on the other hand, can deliver manuscripts that are 100 pages too long, 18 months overdue, and 80% plagiarized, although these, too, are not normal occurrences. But both sides need to ensure that the extremes are covered.

❷ *A contract is biased toward the publisher.* Let's face it: The publisher is out to make money (if it's a commercial house) or at the worst break even (if it's a noncommercial or university press). Publishing any book represents a financial investment—and risk—to a publisher, and it has to do its best to ensure that it doesn't lose its investment. Thus, the publisher structures its contracts to provide itself as much protection as possible. For example, the publisher is going to reserve the rights to determine how the book will be marketed to its audiences or when to put the book out of print, and will generally make it difficult for the author to influence these decisions.

On the other hand, legitimate publishers are not out to defraud their authors. Most scholarly publishers are proud of the service they provide for the exchange of information essential in any free society and want to work with scholars to safeguard that exchange. And on a more prosaic level, word would soon get around about a publisher's unethical practices and drastically prejudice the reputation of the press among future authors and potential customers.

❸ *Don't be afraid to ask questions.* Maybe it stems from a fear of authority, but many potential authors feel that bringing up possible changes in a contract's terms, or asking for a simple explanation about a clause, will spook the publisher. Remember that the publisher is committed to your project as soon as the contract goes out and is not likely to withdraw an offer. It's up to the author to consider and accept the contract.

❹ *Some parts of the contract are negotiable, some are not.* Contracts consist of both boilerplate language, generally drafted for the publisher by lawyers, and specialized provisions, which vary from book to book. The former is often very hard for the publisher to change without going back to the lawyer and incurring legal fees. So any changes in warranties or rights clauses, for example, are often difficult to negotiate. The publisher is more easily able to be flexible on variable provisions. Each publishing house will consider some items sacrosanct . . . that is, unless your book means so much money that it is willing to give up its legal protection. Its degree of contract flexibility generally depends on how important the book is to the house. But never be afraid to question or challenge contract terms.

Parts of a Publishing Contract

Let's look at a fairly standard publishing contract, section by section. There are almost as many different contracts as there are publishers, but the majority will have the following elements in common. In some houses, your acquiring editor will write up and send you the contract. Many publishers, however, have a separate department responsible for administering contracts, and in that case, all your paperwork will be drafted and delivered by an individual there. Be prepared to see anything from a boilerplate contract with the author's name, book title, and other variables typed onto a photocopied form, to a customized contract composed on a word processor and laser printed on fancy bond paper. (By the way, most publishers officially refer to a contract as an "agreement" —it has a more equitable euphony than the sterner "contract.")

Preamble. The introductory section outlines the basics of the agreement. It includes the parties (you and the publisher); the title of the book (remember that the book title is almost always *tentative*—if you or the publisher don't like it, it can be changed now or later); and the length limit of the book (this is almost always *not* tentative—the publisher is probably going to be firm on the length for many reasons).

Rights. When you sign a publishing contract, you are basically giving the publisher the exclusive license to publish and market your work. But extending beyond the book itself can be a group of subsequent rights: translations, book clubs, excerpting parts of the book into other publications, photocopying, microfilming, audio recordings, electronic publishing, even film and TV treatments, to name some of the more common ones. As a rule, a publisher is going to secure all possible subsidiary rights to a work. It will then negotiate deals with all the various foreign publishers, book clubs, photocopy shops, microfilm agents, and the like on behalf of the author. But it's not unheard of for certain authors to initiate subrights deals for their books—a well-traveled scholar occasionally encounters a publisher interested in bringing his wisdom to the German- or Chinese-speaking worlds. Unless you reserve any specific rights for yourself, however, all such deals must be made through the publisher, or they're no deals at all.

Publishers are generally loath to allow authors to retain many rights. Before you ask to reserve some specific rights for yourself, consider whether you believe you can strike a deal with a Spanish-language publisher, or if you really want to cope with copy shops all over the country asking permission to use your chapter in a course pack.

Royalties. In exchange for the above-mentioned rights, the publisher will pay you a percentage of the money collected through sales of the book. This percentage can be computed on either gross or net sales: Gross sales are based on the list price of the book, without discount; net sales are based on the receipts made by the book after discounts are taken (see Chapter 1). The royalty you can expect to receive will range anywhere from 5% to 15%, depending upon such factors as the estimated market size for the book, the success of your previous books, and possible offers from other publishers. For example, you might be able to expect a high royalty if you're doing a textbook with large adoption potential, less if you're writing a specialized or risky book.

The royalties clause will probably also cover other earnings made by the publisher's sales of the subsidiary rights mentioned above, usually at different percentages than the initial book sales. You may get more or less in royalties, depending partly upon how much work the publisher entails for the amount of money involved. One thing to bear in mind: If it isn't in this section, you won't get paid for it. A good way to check to see what you are getting paid for is to compare the rights you are giving away, in the rights section, to the items for which you are receiving royalties, in the royalty section. If the publisher is not paying you for sale of electronic rights, translation rights, or copyright permissions, you should ask why.

Advances. Getting an advance against royalties (money paid in advance of being earned in royalties, to be deducted before royalties are paid to you) is fairly rare in professional or scholarly books; whereas in textbooks, it is more common. If there is going to be an advance, it will likely be paid to you in installments—perhaps one portion at the time the contract is signed, another when the manuscript is delivered to and accepted by the publisher, and the final one upon the book's publication.

Occasionally, publishers provide editorial grants or stipends, cash payments that are *not* subsequently deducted from royalties. Grants most often appear when the author's anticipated out-of-pocket expenses for preparing the manuscript are unusually high—if permission fees are excessive or expensive artwork needs to be drawn, for example.

Payment of Royalties. Frequently, the publisher will describe its procedure for paying out royalties in a separate section of the contract. Once the book has been published and copies are sold, an annual statement will be generated, covering sales since publication or since the previous statement. The royalty check might be enclosed or might arrive a month or two afterwards. Be sure to check the statement and ask your editor any questions you have. If you had any advances, they will probably be deducted from the first royalty statement. In addition, the publisher could reserve a certain amount of your royalties to cover anticipated returns of your book from bookstores.

Manuscript and Publication. Up till now, the contract has been dealing with what the publisher will do for you (publish your book and pay you money for it). Now it's time to discuss what you will do for the publisher: deliver a manuscript that can be affordably produced and sold. The physical aspects of producing a book are discussed here (and also in Chapter 8). The most important points the publisher wants to ensure are for the manuscript to arrive on time and for it to be of publishable quality. The delivery date is vital to the publisher for many reasons. Probably the primary one is that sales projections are made based upon the expected publication date of every book a publisher signs. So it's important that a delivery date be as realistic as possible.

A publisher should have every reason to expect an author to deliver a gem of a manuscript—well organized, well written, with something significant to say. But don't forget the worst-case scenario theory. A contract will often state that the manuscript must be "in content and form satisfactory (or acceptable) to the Publisher." If the manuscript isn't up to the expected standard, and the sponsoring editor feels that nothing can be done to salvage it, the publisher will have the right to cancel the contract. In fact, some publishers will stipulate that the manuscript be favorably reviewed by a group of peers before being accepted for production.

In addition to the manuscript itself, this section will also specify other issues in the production process:

- Additional materials: You'll probably be expected to supply all tables; camera-ready artwork for charts, figures, and maps;

photos; permissions; and also a copy of the manuscript on disk. Don't expect the publisher to automatically pay your copyright permissions fees or create artwork for you.

- Style: The publisher will determine the book's level of copy-editing, design of pages and covers, and printing and binding materials that it feels are most appropriate.
- Index: If there is going to be an index for the book, who is to prepare it? If you don't do it yourself, expect to pay a professional indexer to do it, either one of your own choosing or one supplied by the publisher.
- Page proofs (or galleys): You'll be expected to correct and return proofs promptly. (We'll discuss this in Chapter 8.) If the changes you make to the proofs result in significant typesetting changes, you will probably be required to pay part of the expenses for resetting the pages (yet another worst-case scenario).

Out of Print Provisions. In this section the publisher will describe its procedures with authors in placing books out of print. You will receive written notice, you might be given the option to buy out existing stock at a discount, and ultimately the rights for the book will revert back to you (you might even be given the option of buying the book negatives). Once the rights revert back to you, you have the option of taking your book to another publisher. Pay attention, however, to the way "out of print" is defined. If an alternate edition of the book exists somewhere (say, for example, a foreign language edition or a microfilmed edition), then the book will remain "in print" and the publisher will continue to retain rights.

Force Majeure. This clause prevents the publisher from the proverbial "circumstances beyond its control." If all the copies of the book and the material used to produce it were destroyed by a civil disturbance, or if the government decided to ban all publishing, then the publisher is not liable.

Warranties. Under the warranties clause you will promise that your manuscript is not plagiarized or libelous, and you have not granted any rights that would conflict with those you assign your publisher in the Rights section. It's another clause designed to protect the publisher and, in effect, absolves the publisher of legal responsibility should criminal proceedings or a lawsuit arise out of something in your book. If, for example, your manuscript contained information that a public figure construed as libelous and the figure consequently sued you for damages, the publisher would not be a party to the lawsuit, because you've guaranteed the publisher that the material was not libelous. Moreover, if the publisher gets sued for something that is *your* fault (plagiarism, for example), the publisher can recover its losses from you.

Copyright. The name of the party in whose name the book will be copyrighted will be stated. It's often thought that whosoever name the book is copyrighted in "controls" the book's rights. But there's a big difference between copyright and publishing rights. U. S. copyright laws will protect your work from being used by another party without acknowledging or compensating you or your publisher. Under the publication rights section of the contract, however, you've assigned to your publisher the responsibility of overseeing the subsequent reproduction of your work. So if another publisher wishes to reproduce a table from a book that's been copyrighted in your name, the permission must still be granted by your publisher, who controls the subsidiary rights. Whether you keep the copyright is not really an issue, provided you are protected from wanton use of publishing rights by the publisher, and if you are guaranteed the copyright back when the book goes out of print.

Revisions. Textbooks are most likely to need revised editions—after all, they must be kept up-to-date to reflect new research, fit the changing needs of instruction, and, not least, make used book sales (on which neither the publisher nor the author collects any money) a less viable alternative. If your book has the potential to be adopted by instructors for a class, the publisher will probably include a clause requiring revision of the book on its demand. An out-of-date text can mean loss of sales. This clause may define a timetable for when a revision is due, say, 12 months after the publisher's request. Consider the kind of schedule you feel comfortable with, and make the publisher aware of it.

Special Provisions. Any features out of the ordinary for your project will be covered in this catch-all section. Do you want the publisher to guarantee that special discount for your association? Does the publisher want the mailing list for that association in exchange? Is the book going to be published as part of a series? Will there be contributions by outside authors? If so, those individuals will usually need contracts, too. Will the book be issued in paperback and, if so, when?

Signatures. Here's the bottom line, literally. An actual signature from both parties (usually you and an officer of the publishing company) is required. Most publishers will send the contract without a signature; in that case sign *all* of the copies sent you and send *all* of them back. The publisher will then look them over, sign, and return a copy to you for reference. (Yes, even this most simple part of the contract process occasionally stumps Ph.D.s everywhere.)

The concluding section will usually sum up with a statement that the agreement is binding, not only on you and the publisher, but also on your respective successors/heirs and legal representatives. Generally, the publisher will retain the power to assign rights to a third party—for example, another publisher. This is usually one of the nonnegotiable clauses, because a publisher's list of future contracts is the house's chief asset if the owners ever want to sell the company. However, your obligations to the publisher in the contract cannot be assigned to any third party. For example, you can't get someone to ghostwrite the book for you. Also mentioned will be the state whose laws will be used to interpret the contract (usually the publisher's home state). This is important in the unfortunate occurrence of a lawsuit between you and your publisher. In an attempt to keep disputes out of court, many publishers are now including a contract clause insisting on legal arbitration in cases of dispute.

It's all set in stone now, right? Not necessarily. If a modification of the contract's terms becomes necessary down the line, you and your publisher can always agree on an *addendum* to the original (quite simply, an addition to the contract). If you find you just can't make that delivery date, or really need to get an advance to pay for your research assistant, an addendum can be issued to cover these unforeseen issues once you and the publisher verbally agree.

Ask the Editor

As we said earlier, it doesn't hurt to raise issues after the contract is in your hands. Every detail of the publishing process can't be covered in the preliminary discussions with your editor, and many are probably not in the contract. Some issues worth bringing up are:

- Noncompetition: Some publishers will ask you not to write a book that will compete with the book you are writing for them. You need to ask them to define—on paper—what they mean by "competing."
- Design: Will you have any say at all about the inside and outside design of the book? If you have strong feelings about the color of the cover, or don't want other books advertised on the back cover, ask if you can have input on design.
- Editions: Will your book also be published in paperback (or hardcover)? Unless it is stated outright, the publisher isn't obligated to produce both versions of your book.

Once again: If it concerns you, bring it up. The publisher may have made the best offer it feels it can, but it will not retract an offer because you ask questions. So be inquisitive, and don't stop until you are satisfied with the answers.

Everybody Wins

The contract phase is the first "official" dealing you will have with your publisher. The communication you and your publisher have at this stage can be indicative of the communication you will have throughout the rest of the process. So the earlier and the clearer you can express your desires, even your anxieties about what will happen in the publishing process, the better. Any negotiator knows that the outcome of a truly successful negotiation is not to have one side repress another; rather, both sides should walk away from the table better off than when they approached. Both you and the publisher have vested interests in a project, and the contract should ensure that both your interests are satisfied.

Summary

Even though the contract may look daunting to the uninitiated, it is seldom necessary to get the advice of a lawyer to interpret it for you. Read the various sections of the contract carefully. Examine what rights you are giving to the publisher and what royalties you are getting in exchange. Make sure you understand the warranties clause, and scrutinize the special provisions section closely. Finally, remember that even though such sections as the warranties are seldom negotiable, other sections may be. And don't hesitate to ask your editor or the contracts administrator for clarification on any points. After all, neither you nor your editor wants any misunderstandings that will hurt your relationship down the line or hinder the development and publication of your book.

And speaking of your relationship with your editor, in the next chapter we will explore how you, as a signed author, can get the most out of that relationship.

7 | Getting the Most Out of Your Editor

Now let's talk about getting your book published, which is a different story from getting a contract. This chapter tells how to get the most out of your publisher—particularly, your editor—once you've signed a contract. For now, we'll discuss only the period between contract signature and manuscript completion. Chapters 8 and 9 will explain how your book is copyedited, printed, and sold.

It is difficult to get accurate statistics concerning the number of cancelled contracts, because authors and publishing houses are loath to discuss projects that were signed but never printed. Word-of-mouth estimates and the ever-present grapevine, however, indicate that more than 15% of *signed* books never become *actual* books. This chapter provides some practical advice so that your book doesn't fall into this never-never land.

On a more positive note, most projects do get published, and a careful reading of this chapter will give you some ideas on how to make the most of the experience. There are no set rules—just guidelines and tips for getting the most out of your editor. Follow this advice and you are far more likely to stay on schedule, write a better book, and find the experience rewarding. You might even want to write another book.

What You Can Expect From Your Editor

Your editor's job is just beginning once the ink on the contract is dry. It's his responsibility (let's assume this editor is a man) to make sure that your book has a safe journey from your word processor to the marketplace. You should take advantage of this ongoing relationship and get as much input as possible from your editor. Above all, don't be bashful in asking him about providing the services described in this chapter—providing them is his job.

Establishing a Plan for Outside Reviews

You shouldn't have to write in a vacuum. All kinds of books need outside critical commentary from your peers. Textbooks need reviews that check the manuscript's accuracy, timeliness, and appropriateness for its market. Scholarly monographs need reviews that verify the manuscript's credentials as an authoritative, state-of-the-art statement on a particular topic. "Practitioner" or "how to" books need reviews that confirm the manuscript's usefulness for its audience.

These reviews are quite different from the reviews that your editor probably commissioned earlier, when he or she was deciding whether to offer you a contract. Back then, your editor was trying to determine if you were on the right track. The postcontractual manuscript reviews, carried out as you are actually writing the first and second drafts, usually are a great deal more detailed and are designed to give you more specific feedback to assist you in completing a final draft.

These reviews can be critical to your book's success. Without your peers' input, you could spend a lot of time writing to an audience that isn't there. Make sure you work with your editor to ensure that:

- your manuscript is being reviewed
- it is being reviewed by people with appropriate backgrounds (and you should feel free to talk with your editor about what those backgrounds should be)

- you both have a clear idea of when these reviews will be carried out and when you will be expected to receive them and respond to them
- you both have an opportunity to discuss each review and your reactions to it

Establishing a Schedule

Establishing a schedule for completing chapters may even seem more basic than knowing your review schedule, but in fact, your writing schedule revolves around the plan for obtaining outside reviews.

First, work with your editor to make sure that your project will be reviewed. Then, decide by whom. Next, figure out when you both want to get this feedback. Do you want it after you've written just a few chapters, so a reviewer might catch something you can avoid in later chapters? Or would you rather finish a first draft, then get reviewer feedback all at once for you to fold into a second draft? There's no right or wrong answer, but you need to talk this over with your editor, plan the review process, and then determine the overall writing schedule.

Get an Author's Guide

Most publishers have an "Author's Guide," a manual that explains their standards for manuscript preparation, writing style, word-processing formats, and other points. Ask for it, then follow its guidelines religiously. You'll save yourself a lot of time later, and probably help to get your book through production faster (see Chapter 8). For example, you might find the publisher wants your references in APA style rather than the Chicago style that you usually use. Or that the publisher requests that the entire manuscript, including quotations and references, be double-spaced.

Use Your Editor's Eyes and Ears

While you're writing, your editor won't be sitting back at headquarters, waiting patiently for you to finish your manuscript. He will be attending seminars and conferences, visiting college campuses, reading professional books and journals, and talking to other authors and reviewers. Some editors are as well networked as the authors who are writing books for them.

Learn to use your editor as a resource. Let him be your eyes and ears in the field while you work on your manuscript. Do you want to know what's going on at universities on the West Coast? Ask your editor. Do you want to know what were the hot buzzwords at the ABC conference last week (the one you couldn't get to because you were slaving away on the book)? Ask your editor. Need the scoop on a hot new book that's just come out in the market that you're aiming at with your manuscript? Ask your editor.

Never hesitate to pick up the phone to bounce some ideas around with your editor. In many ways an editor is like a bonus reviewer. He might know your book's target audience even better than you do. Use your editor to help you keep your finger on the pulse of your marketplace.

Face-to-Face Meetings

Keep in touch with your editor so you can take advantage of any opportunities to have a face-to-face meeting to discuss progress, reviews, or any matters of interest. If he is visiting your area, make it clear that you'd like to meet just to talk things over. Even if you don't have any earthshaking news to impart, you should let your editor know that you want to be called upon if he's in the area.

The same goes if you are going to be in your publisher's neighborhood. Call ahead and suggest a meeting. It's your editor's job to put his expertise at your disposal.

There's potentially more to be gained than just an update. If you "bond" with your editor, he will be more likely to champion your book throughout the entire publishing company. You get the chance to provide direct input on your book and its audience—information that your editor can later feed to the marketing and production staff. On the other side of the coin, you can expect your editor to be willing to talk about the book and *his* expectations.

Who knows? Your editor could end up being your friend, and certainly the communication and interaction will do much to help you write the book of your dreams.

What You Should Do for Your Editor

You have some responsibilities of your own as an author. Here's what you can do to not only make your editor's life easier but also improve your project's chances for success.

Keep in Touch

Editors hate surprises. Keep your editor informed about good news, bad news, any news. Most important, keep your editor up-to-date on your schedule. If you're keeping up, fine— but remember to let your editor know. If you're not keeping up, let your editor know right away.

Why is this so important? Because while you're writing, the publisher is making plans based both on the dates the books under development are scheduled to go to market and on their projected sales. And in some cases, publishing deadlines are very time dependent. The introduction of major textbooks must correspond to the adoption season; publication of an annual series, or publication of series volumes in batches (as this series is published) are time sensitive. In other cases, more flexibility can be set into deadlines and scheduling. Still, publishers build budgets based upon the expectation that certain books will arrrive at certain times. With enough advance warning, schedules often can be juggled.

So, if that Fulbright you were hoping for came through, tell your editor as soon as possible. While no one likes to hear bad news, it's better than his trying to contact you when the manuscript is due, only to find out that you're in the Amazon rain forest for the next 6 months and don't have a forwarding address.

You have at your disposal lots of ways to keep in touch. Mail, phone, fax, voice mail, E-mail—all of them do the job. You should probably experiment with some or all of them until you find the one that seems to establish the friendliest and most timely relationship between you and your editor. All it takes is a direct question: "What's the best way for me to get hold of you?"

Provide Early Notice About Shifts in Focus

If you are planning a major shift in emphasis, one that differs significantly from your original proposal, you should definitely discuss your plans with your editor before veering off in a new direction. Remember, editors hate surprises, and there's no worse surprise than finding out that the manuscript *delivered* is not the manuscript *promised*.

Shifts in a book's focus, or even audience, are not rare. Sometimes, after you have read a batch of reviews, drastic shifts might even appear to be necessary. Just don't go off in a new direction without notifying your editor and getting his assent. Otherwise, you may find yourself holding the bag at the end of the project, with a manuscript that your editor doesn't want to publish.

Stay Flexible

Stay true to your vision for your book, but don't get so wedded to it that you remain blind to necessary changes. Reviews can be harsh, but often they reveal opportunities for improvement. Your editor can often seem like a cruel task-master, but remember that he is usually your biggest fan, who, like you, is only trying to publish the best possible book. So when your work is being questioned, or when you don't seem to be getting your own way, try to stay loose and open to new ideas. Your editor has the same goal as you do.

Three Key Tips

Here are three facts of life about publishing companies that you should know. The first is just a helpful reminder; the other two can be critical under certain circumstances.

1. Allow for "Editorial Letdown"

What is "Editorial Letdown"? It's what happens to your editor right after you've signed the contract for your manuscript. He has already spent a lot of time championing your project to an editorial board and will probably be strutting with pride around headquarters after you've signed on the dotted line. The tendency is to sit back and savor the moment and to think that the job is done. In fact, the job is only just beginning.

Now it's time to get the manuscript off to a good start by setting a schedule and selecting reviewers. This is no time for your editor to be basking in glory, or to think that you won't be needing his attention for a while. But the phenomenon of Editorial Letdown sometimes results in exactly that.

You'll never get any editor to admit to having Editorial Letdown. In fact, we're coining the phrase in this book. Just know that it exists in the real world.

What can you do about it? First, acknowledge that it exists. If you find that your editor does not seem quite as attentive after you've signed a contract as before, you've spotted a symptom of Editorial Letdown. It probably will pass, so don't take it personally. You are probably better off letting your editor having his few days of glory, then using a gentle reminder to say, "Now it's time to get to the **real** task of producing a superior book." That should get your editor's attention.

If you never spot the signs of Editorial Letdown, consider yourself fortunate and concentrate on the advice given earlier in this chapter for getting the most out of your relationship with your editor. If the warning signs show up and are persistent, then you'll have to be persistent and work with your editor until he comes around and provides the support services mentioned earlier in this chapter.

2. *Expand Your Contacts Within Your Publishing Company*

Your editor, although important, isn't the only person who can help you with your project. As your manuscript develops, take time to get to know the following people:

Your Editor's Assistant (often referred to as the EA). This person usually handles the day-to-day details of your manuscript's review process and probably will help prepare it for production. The EA is almost always more accessible by phone than your editor, and might be more helpful when you have quick questions. A good EA can probably tell you more about what is really going on inside the publishing house than the editor can or will. Get to know him or her well.

Your Editor's Boss. You might get a chance to meet this person (who is usually an Executive Editor or Editor-in-Chief) at a conference or at the publisher's headquarters. Use the opportunity to get a sense of that person's vision for the publisher, and also to describe your own project. Support for your book at this level never hurts, and the boss could provide crucial continuity for you in the event your editor leaves.

Your Publisher's Production Staff. You won't need to work with them in any detail until the manuscript is completed (Chapter 8), but if you get a chance to meet them beforehand, take advantage of it. Ask them what you'll need to do when you ultimately submit the manuscript for copyediting and type-setting—you could learn something that will save you a lot of time and effort later on. And the goodwill you earn will pay off when your book becomes their "baby."

Your Publisher's Product or Promotion Manager for Books in Your Area. This person (usually a member of the Marketing Department) will plan your book's marketing campaign and write the advertising copy. Now's the time to get this person turned on to your manuscript. Any information you can feed the promotion manager on the uniqueness of your project, on your main ideas, and on the audience will result in better advertising copy and more targeted mailings later.

Your Local Sales Representative. If your publisher has sales representatives (most academic/professional publishers do not, but textbook publishers do), your local representative can be useful in providing you with information on your potential readers, on competing books, and on events inside the publishing house.

3. Keep Records of All Communication With Your Publisher

We make this recommendation with the hope that you'll never have to use it. One always hopes that a partner—and the publisher/author relationship is a partnership—will keep all promises. People move around in the publishing business (as in most professions), however, and sometimes authors have to deal with a new editor, or even a whole new management team.

When that happens, you will want to have a record of exactly what commitments your publisher has made to you. We're not suggesting that an editor or publisher will automatically be trying to change the rules of the game; in fact, in times of turnover, publishers usually tend toward maintaining the status quo. By keeping careful records of what's supposed to be happening with your manuscript, you'll be doing the new regime a big favor. Without the time to read through every file and phone log, a new editor will be happy to have you fill him in on the current status of your project.

And if new personnel do want to change the program, yours and your editor's written words are valuable insurance for you. For example, your editor's verbal assurance 2 years ago to pay $2,000 in permissions fees will conflict with a belt-tightening policy today, and your assertion that your editor orally guaranteed payment will, in all likelihood, fall on deaf ears. A letter from your editor, however, agreeing to pay the permission fees is legally binding on the new editor or administration.

Don't Forget Your Editor
When the Manuscript Is Complete

Once your manuscript is complete and safe in the hands of your publisher's production department, it's easy to forget about your acquisitions editor. You're thinking that he is out trying to sign up a new generation of books and doesn't care about you now that your book is in production. You have a production editor who'll take care of everything from here on in. Wrong.

Now more than ever you should be keeping in close touch with your editor. He has to represent the book to the publisher's marketing personnel, and you'll want to have some say in that process. Find out what you can do to help your book's performance. What conferences should you be attending? Who do you know who should see a copy of the book? What key points about the book should be highlighted in its advertising? Who should be approached for testimonials? Chapter 9 says a lot more about book marketing, and what you can do to help. Just remember that your editor has a lot to do with that effort, and be prepared to offer your assistance.

This is also the best time to discuss new book ideas with your editor. Chances are you have been thinking about spin-offs, revisions, or other book possibilities while finishing up your current project. Sometimes the things you have to toss out of a manuscript would work in another kind of book project. Your editor should always be looking for new book ideas—now is the time to discuss yours with him, while they're fresh in your mind, and your working relationship is still active. Even if you don't want to get working right away on a new project, it's a good time to share ideas and make plans.

What to Do if Your Editor Leaves

First of all, don't panic. It could matter enormously. Or not at all. Editorial turnover is a fairly frequent occurrence in the publishing industry. Fortunately, it happens often enough that we can identify some positive steps for you to take that will soften the blow—perhaps even strengthen your project in the long run.

If you have done a good job of expanding your base of contacts within your publisher, it shouldn't be the end of the world if your editor has left the company. You will still have a loyal fan club within your publisher, and there should be no breakdown in communication.

Also, if you have done a good job of keeping records of all author/publisher communication, now would be a good time to bring them out and reread them. Your previous editor wasn't just making personal commitments—he was committing the entire company to a course of action. That should not change just because you have a new editor.

The best thing you can do if your editor leaves is form a bond with the new kid on the block. Remember that the new editor will be trying to leave his own personal mark on the company as quickly as possible. Now's the time for you to be talking to the new editor about "our" book project. Forget about the previous editor and start showing the new editor how you want to work together to make your book a success for him.

You might even want to try finding out what, if any, new mandate has been handed to the new editor. (Here's where your network of contacts within your publisher could come in handy.) Perhaps he has been installed to bring in some hot new books, and can be convinced that your book is indeed a hot prospect. Or perhaps the new editor has been charged with taking better care of books already under contract, and thus will appreciate hearing from you that you are eager to receive editorial guidance. Whatever it is, try to identify the best hook into your new editor's attention.

Thus, if you've built a network of contacts in the publishing house, or if the new editor is sympathetic to your project, you can continue with business as usual. In other cases, however, the change of editor orphans the ex-editor's projects. These unwanted leftovers rarely receive the same kind of attention and support around the publishing house as those that have the original editor to champion them. We all know horror stories of authors who have gone through three or four different editors at a press, each with different ideas for where the book should be going, and with little notion of what the book was really trying to do.

If your relationship with the press is highly dependent on your editor, it is (rarely) put into the contract that you can break it if the editor leaves. Sometimes, even without a contractual clause, you can withdraw your book by negotiating with the new editor. Usually, however, you will have to rebuild the relationship with someone new and hope for the best.

One final suggestion: Chances are your past editor will resurface someday at another publisher. So, if you're still on speaking terms, stay close to your ex-editor, and you might be building a contact for the future.

Summary

During the period between your signature on a contract and your manuscript's transmittal to your publisher's production department, your key contact person is your editor. It's important at this stage to think of your editor as a resource person. When you were seeking a contract from your publisher, you had to sell your editor on your manuscript. Now you must shift and use your editor's experience and skill to your project's advantage. The key is good, open-ended communication. Editors and publishers hate surprises. You should, too. Keep the lines of communication open, and your book will survive almost anything that can happen along the way.

Above all, treat the author/editor relationship as a partnership. Take a look at the top authors and publishers in any discipline, and you'll see that the best ones stick together. Publishers stay loyal to their favorite authors, and authors stay loyal to their favorite publishers. These relationships take hard work, but the books that result reap the rewards.

8 | The Production Process

Your completed manuscript represents many months of intensive labor on your part, as well as extensive help and encouragement on the part of your editor. It has gone through two, perhaps more, drafts, but it is finally complete. The next step is for your book to go into production. Production does not mean that your manuscript is propelled into a black hole to emerge evolved, a printed and bound book. And although a production crew might now and then approach warp speed, producing a book is a process. In good publishing houses, this process is usually logical, organized, and efficient. Sometimes not. As an author, however, you can either fuel the success of the process or help turn the production of your book into a nightmare for you and the production staff.

A Point to Remember

During the production process, you will be dealing with a team of professionals who have seen hundreds, even thousands of manuscripts and have successfully processed millions of printed characters. As you deal with production staff, it is important to keep this in mind: They do know what they are doing. Usually.

Occasionally, however, you will encounter production "professionals" who don't seem to know what they're doing. Either way, it pays for you to know the various steps of book production and some of the pitfalls that await the unwary. The purpose of this chapter is to give you the information you need to work successfully with a production staff, competent or inept.

Before Your Manuscript Is in Your Publisher's Hands

Some of the most important things you can do to make the production process go more smoothly need to be done long before you print out the final copy of your manuscript to send to your publisher. By anticipating what the production staff will want from you, you can make their life—and yours—considerably easier.

So, what exactly do they want from you? At some point, your publisher probably sent you an "Author's Guide" or other detailed guidelines for preparing your manuscript, mentioned briefly in the previous chapter. If you have read, understood, and followed to the letter the publisher's manuscript preparation guidelines, you'll be giving the production staff what they need to produce your book efficiently. Generally, these guidelines include the following:

- at least one, perhaps two, clean copies of the manuscript
- double-spaced manuscript printed on one side only
- disk that matches the manuscript character-for-character
- written permission for quotations and other material, such as tables and artwork, that are protected by copyright
- camera-ready artwork for any figures, charts, maps, line drawings, and sometimes, tables (we'll explain the term *camera-ready* a little later)
- references/bibliography in the correct referencing style, such as APA (American Psychological Association), MLA (Modern Language Association), Chicago (*The Chicago Manual of Style*), or

perhaps a special "house" style, for which the publisher should provide you a detailed style sheet
- full address, phone numbers, fax numbers, bitnet or E-mail numbers for yourself and all other authors or contributors

No matter how insignificant or even arcane these manuscript specifications seem, the prudent author meets them. They really do affect the time it takes to produce your manuscript, as well as how you are viewed by the production team. For example, if you think that the details of reference style don't matter much, spend several tedious hours with a copy editor trying to transpose legibly words, move commas and periods, fix capitalization, add or delete underlines, query discrepancies, and generally clean up 30 pages of carelessly prepared references. Apart from the time added to the production schedule, do you really want to reduce the person entrusted with editing your work to a snarling pit bull?

If, on the other hand, you demonstrate that you cared enough about the production of your manuscript to follow the publisher's guidelines, this could very well translate into a production team predisposed to giving your book the attention, care, and priority you feel it deserves. In all stages of the publishing process, it pays to have the publishing team on your side. Face it: If two projects sit on a production editor's desk, one with problems and one that's a pleasure to work on, which one will the editor be inclined to pick up first? You want it to be yours.

One Final Check

When you think that you've prepared your manuscript with the care of a professional—and if your deadline allows it—set it aside for a few days. Then give the entire manuscript one final reading, double-checking the points covered in the publisher's guidelines. Make any necessary corrections, with the same care you took to write the manuscript, before giving the grateful production team the cleanest, easiest-to-publish manuscript possible.

The Production Process

So, you've sent off your perfect, complete manuscript and have met your deadline. Your most important contact will be a production editor or similarly titled person who will shepherd the book through the production process. As suggested in earlier chapters, it is useful to build a good working relationship with this person, because the production editor can either help or hinder the smooth flow of the publication process and the extent of your control over it.

At this point many authors imagine that their work is finished. In fact, a great deal remains to be done both by the production staff and by the author. Figure 8.1 shows the general production process for a scholarly book. Each publisher may alter the order of the steps involved and perhaps the language used to describe them, but most come close to the procedure shown in the figure.

The Production Schedule

Each publisher has its own ideal schedule, a sample of which is shown in Figure 8.2. Books can take up to a year (or longer) to produce or, when necessary, the time can be compressed to accommodate a tight schedule. At Sage Publications, for example, the norm is 6 months, though one important book went from manuscript into 200 camera-ready pages in 13 days. In any event, much of the production time for each manuscript is spent waiting in queue—for the production editor, copy editor, keyboarder, or printer. Each publisher also tries to minimize this wait time, because it is spending money on the book without hope of recouping it until the book is in print. To the extent that you can respond to the publisher's

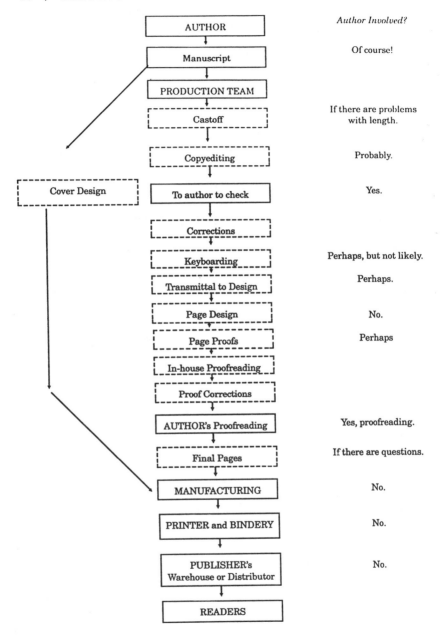

Figure 8.1. The Production Process

inquiries and keep to the deadlines imposed on you, you can help minimize this waiting time and get your book produced as quickly as possible.

Design and Castoff

Book design is the crucial process of devising a format that will present your work in an aesthetically pleasing, readable, and functional way. From a range of type styles, page formats, and other design elements, the book designer creates the format for your book.

One of the important factors the designer must take into account is the projected length of the book, which directly affects production costs. Consequently, once a basic design has been specified a "castoff," or a page character count, is done that provides an estimate of the length, given the typographical specifications for your book. With this information, the book designer can decide whether to adjust the design to stretch or compact your text so that it meets the desired number of printed pages. It is not unusual to add an extra point of leading (white space) between lines in order to increase the number of pages, or to condense the manuscript by changing type specifications. Unless your manuscript casts off significantly over or under the mark, you'll probably hear nothing about this step in the process.

This degree of flexibility is nice, but there are limits to the amount of expanding or contracting the designer can do. It is rare that an 800-page manuscript will compress to 200 printed pages, despite the best efforts of the designer. So, while you are not always expected to produce the exact number of words or manuscript pages called for by the contract, the tolerance for overages or underages is limited. That is one key reason why you should come as close to the length specified by the contract as you can: Trying to cut the manuscript when it is already in production is a hassle for you and will lengthen the production schedule severely.

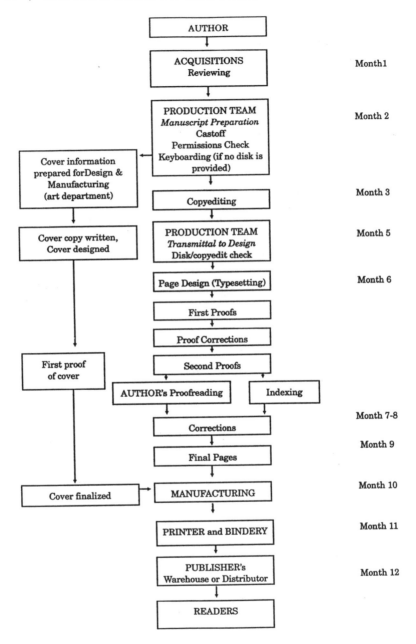

Figure 8.2. Production Timeline

Copyediting

While the book designer specifies the appearance of your book, a copy editor labors over the final form of your words. In copyediting, every character of your manuscript is read with care. Generally speaking, an academic copy editor's job is to ensure that the text is correct in such details as grammar, punctuation, spelling and matters of editorial style, such as the treatment of numbers, abbreviations, and capitalizations. Your in-text reference citations will be carefully compared with your full reference list, and any discrepancies queried to you either in writing or by phone.

You may be asked to research and supply answers regarding references that are incomplete, contradictory, or confusing. The sooner you're able to respond, the sooner your manuscript can move on to the next step in the production process. To anticipate these problems, it is a good idea to keep the notes on your references handy after you submit the manuscript.

While correcting errors and ensuring consistency are the copy editor's core functions, in some cases more extensive editing will be done for clarity, flow, tone, and other points of writing style. The extent of the editing done during production varies from publisher to publisher and from project to project. To avoid surprises, try to get as clear an idea as you can from the publisher about the level of editing projected for your book. Also, make sure you ask your production editor *before* the editing begins whether you will be reviewing the copyedited manuscript, as publishers' policies differ. In scholarly publishing, the author might not see the edited manuscript before it is set in type when the editing is limited to routine corrections and occasional rewriting of muddy sentences and the like. If the editing is more extensive, as it typically is in textbooks and some scholarly manuscripts, you will probably be sent the edited manuscript so that you can review the editing and respond to the copy editor's queries.

Whatever the extent of the editing, the copy editor's job is to smooth the reader's way through the text and prevent irritating and embarrassing errors while preserving your meaning and voice. It's natural to be somewhat defensive when soemone else changes your words, but good copy editors, like good reviewers, have your best interests in mind. If you don't understand why a change has been made, you have a perfect right to ask. By the same token, if you want a change in the editing, be prepared to explain why. In all cases, do your best to be objective.

Whether you review the edited manuscript or are only contacted by phone to resolve reference questions and the like, be as prompt as you can in your response. The sooner you resolve any issues that come up in copyediting, the sooner your manuscript can move on to the next step in the production process. And if you do review the copyedited manuscript, do so with care. Changes later on will be far less welcome—and extensive changes in proofs could even cost you money if the publisher uses an outside compositor, or typesetter, to prepare the finished pages.

Keyboarding

Once the copyedited manuscript is complete and your responses to queries have been incorporated, the next step is to convert the typed characters of the manuscript into typeset pages. In the transformation to computerized publishing, most manuscripts, at some point or another, are put into electronic form. If you could not supply a computer disk (or did not use a computer to write the book), the "hard copy" (meaning the printed pages of your manuscript) will be typed, or keyboarded, into a computer. Along with your text, typemarking codes may be inserted by the copy editor or keyboarder that will, in turn, translate into the appropriate type specifications when your disk is processed into printed pages.

Typesetting

Traditionally, books were *typeset*, turned from manuscript into publishable form by the publisher using some form of typographic equipment. In most publishing houses today, typesetting is a term no longer appropriate. Desktop publishing allows text already on computer disk to be poured into one of many typographic molds preset in the computer, separating the functions of keyboarding (typing characters onto disk) from typesetting (designing and arranging the format in which these characters will be played out, according to the formula worked out by the book designer).

The present-day text designer merely arranges and codes the material already on disk. The size of a subhead is determined, as well as the typeface, placement, and spacing above and below each head. The same holds true for every other element in your manuscript: chapter titles, references, quotations, footnotes, figure and table captions, table text, and so on. Each element carries a code that translates into the appropriate typeface, size, and spacing. Changes in the code will result in changes in the final look of the typeset page.

Page Proofs

Before desktop publishing revolutionized page production, the next step in the process was called *galley proofs*, the term used for long sheets of paper on which the edited and typeset manuscript was printed for inspection before the material was broken into pages. In contrast, today's proofs are usually *page proofs*, which represent what the final pages of your book should look like.

Most publishers like the author to inspect the pages of the book-in-process for errors at least once. Very often, these page proofs will come with little warning due to the timing uncertainties of the production process. Some authors are convinced that proofs always arrive during finals week, on Christmas Eve, or on the day before their long-planned vacation to Maui.

Publisher deadlines for returning the page proofs are usually tight. You should have 1 to 3 weeks to proofread the typeset pages. If you are given more time, question whether you've been bumped in the production schedule. If you are given less time, buckle down. And know that, in many cases, it is a negotiable item for the publisher. If your grant deadline is the same as the publisher's proofing deadline, the publisher will usually wait if it knows in advance when the corrected proofs are to be expected.

To make your book the best it can be, set aside enough time to read your proofs thoroughly. Many hands have touched your manuscript since its arrival in-house, and errors can—and do—occur along the way. This is your opportunity to make certain your book is letter-perfect.

Read your pages for typographical errors. If your book contains math, check each equation against your manuscript. If you have spoken with the copy editor about awkward passages but have not seen the edited manuscript, check the editor's corrections. Don't take anything for granted, including the title of the book and the spelling of your name.

Either before you receive page proofs or simultaneous to it, proofs are also being read in the publisher's production department or by a free-lance proofreader. Many of the errors you note on your set of proofs will also be caught by the publisher's proofreader. In most cases, even when an author is extremely conscientious about the proofs, this proofreader will find even more errors. That is, after all, the proofreader's job.

As you note corrections on your page proofs, remember that now is *not* the time to rewrite your book. Now is not the time to rewrite even a chapter of your book. Now is the time to correct, not to create. In fact, most publishers will charge you for excessive changes, those beyond correcting typographical errors. Whatever deadline you have been given in returning your proofs to the publisher, it is critical to *meet it*. Unless a publisher's production is sloppy or ill-planned, deadlines are not set arbitrarily. Each project (and there might be hundreds) is wedged between variables—personnel, free-lance accessibility, print schedules—usually just as tightly choreographed as a dance. Unless you have a valid reason (deaths or births sometimes qualify), if you miss a proof deadline, your book might miss the time frame allowed and will have to wait for the next available slot.

Proof Corrections

The production editor who has been shepherding your book through every stage of production will now inspect every proof correction called for, both yours and the proofreader's, determining whether the correction is legitimate and necessary, and making sure the necessary ones are made.

Unless you have very few corrections noted on your set of proofs, you can expect to hear from a production editor. Sometimes notations are ambiguous or made improperly, sometimes they're illegible, and sometimes they don't seem to make sense. The production editor will call you when he or she has questions about a correction you've requested. Again, make sure that you remain accessible during this critical stage.

Keep in mind that your production editor is usually a pro and knows style and substance, house rules, and the times when these rules should be circumvented. The production editor's goal is the same as yours: to get your book as close to perfect as it can be.

Indexing

Most scholarly books have either a single index or separate author and subject indexes. In some fields, other indexes are expected: lists of original documents, biblical or classical citations, archival sources used, and so on. Because indexes are tools often used by readers, researchers, and students, it pays to make sure that they are accurate and thorough.

Most often, the author is asked either to provide the index(es) or to arrange (and/or pay) for the indexing. Author indexes—a list of all authors' names mentioned in the text and the pages on which they appear—are fairly mechanical to prepare. Subject indexes are far more complex—and more difficult to give to a student, spouse, or colleague to do—because they require a good understanding of the material. These indexes require you to develop a list of *descriptors*, develop a hierarchy of them (i.e., the descriptor "subject index" would be a subset of the category "index"), and then fill in the page numbers where these terms or concepts appear.

Most scholarly authors find preparing an index the most difficult part of the book production process. Hiring a professional indexer is one solution to this problem. Indexers can sometimes be found locally; otherwise, you can locate them through the American Society of Indexers (see Additional Resources section for the address). If you hire an indexer, be sure the arrangements are made in advance, because indexing time will be short—usually no more than a couple of weeks.

If you choose to prepare the index yourself, be aware that with the scheduled publication date approaching, the publisher is not likely to allow you very much time. The process can be somewhat shortened if you prepare your list of authors and descriptors in advance, so that you only need to insert page numbers when the page proofs for indexing arrive. While the index can be a difficult task, console yourself that the book is almost finished.

Final Pages

When you complete the index and correction decisions have been made, the proofs that have been marked by the production editor now return to the text designer. Errors are corrected, indexes are inserted at the end, the text is poured back into the typographical mold, and the final pages are printed. In the days before laser printers, all of the book's pages were pasted up individually on boards, or *flats*, to be photographed so that printing plates could be made from the negatives. Now, high-resolution laser printers produce camera-ready pages of your text, complete with "crop marks" to guide the printer. This stage may be called a variety of things at different publishing houses—final repro (reproduction proofs), camera-ready pages, final boards, or final pages. Whatever these proofs are called, they provide the precise image from which the printing plates will be made.

Sometimes the publisher will allow you to inspect a copy of the final, camera-ready pages prior to printing. If you are doing this, remember that the only obstacle between your book and the printer is *you*. Respond with all due haste. You should expect this inspection anywhere from 1 to 4 weeks after you've returned your proof correction set. More commonly, the publisher is unwilling to send you another set of proofs because of cost and scheduling reasons. Thus, discuss with the production editor any corrections that are absolutely crucial or changes that are complex and might be misinterpreted, and, if necessary, insist on seeing only those specific items again.

Your production editor personally checks each page in its final form again, comparing the requested correction to the result on the page, checking page numbers, making sure that the type is sharp enough for good reproduction, and giving the entire book one last appraisal. When the editor is satisfied that every element is in order, the final pages are delivered to the printer.

The Cover

Concurrent with the manuscript's production, a designer has been working on your book's cover. Before computer-aided graphics, producing a cover mechanical (the actual art from which the printer will work) was time-consuming and tedious. While your cover designer might initially use hand-drawn sketches, most now turn to the computer to generate fast—and extremely creative—design options.

By the time your book is in final pages, the cover designer has produced a *mechanical*, a version of the design that includes detailed instructions to the printer about the color of ink, overlays, screens, or any other special effects. This final art is pasted up on a *board*, a stiff paper that allows for easy handling without damaging the artwork itself.

Your publisher might allow your input on the design, color, or typography of the cover. If so, this would have been negotiated at the contract stage (see Chapter 6) of the process.

At the Printer

Very few publishers print their own books. Instead, publishers turn to printers, usually via the publisher's in-house print buyer, who contracts with one of hundreds of outside book printers. Once the final pages and the cover have been delivered to the printer, a whole new team takes over.

The publisher's print buyer has given detailed instructions regarding the print run (number of copies to print), stock (type of paper), binding on the cover (saddle-stitched, Smyth-sewn, hot glue, and so on), page alignment, and special treatments (photographs or plates) that the printer will follow. Just as computers have significantly accelerated the production process, they have also affected the printing industry. Some printers now produce pages through a transfer of data from a computer disk directly to the printing plates, eliminating the tedious process of shooting photographic negatives of each page. Most printers, however, still shoot "negs," make a printing plate, then position all the plates into page *signatures*, usually a multiple of eight pages, that are folded and collated for binding after they come off the press.

Whether the printer handles the actual binding in-house or sends the printed signatures out to a separate bindery, during the binding process, the signatures are attached to printed covers. The finished products (bound books) are packed into boxes and shipped to the publisher's warehouse for distribution.

After the Fact

Even when the final copy of your book is in your hands, your job is not over. As you review your book, you might find errors you missed during proofs. You should note these in detail. Most publishers will keep track of such errors and make the changes prior to reprinting your book.

What Can Go Wrong

So far, we've been assuming that your publisher's production team is made up of professionals, people who know what they are doing and have your interest at heart. Suppose, for a moment, that this is not the case.

A Worst-Case Scenario

You've done your part. The manuscript and disk, prepared to exacting standards, have been delivered to your publisher on schedule. It's time to kick back, take your shoes off, and . . . Is that the phone?

"I'm terribly sorry, Dr. Trusting, but we can't seem to find Chapters 7 and 13, and page 201 is missing."

And 2 months into production: "Hi, Dr. Trusting, we just discovered that you're 100 pages too long for your contract. Can you please cut out two chapters?"

And it goes on:

The editor loses your disk.

The copy editor substitutes "intra" for "inter," completely changing the meaning of your entire book.

The editor inadvertently substitutes your ex's last name, which you haven't used for 5 years, on the title page.

It can be an author's worst nightmare—all the horror stories you've ever heard about publishing, rolled into one horror story, and it's yours.

How to Avoid Catastrophe

Catastrophe *can* be avoided, provided you are prepared for contingencies:

❶ First, keep copies of everything—a copy of your manuscript, disks, all permissions forms, all tables and figures, and the index. Everything.

❷ Label everything carefully. Put your name and the book's title on your manuscript and all other items you send to the publisher. Put your disks and photos in labeled envelopes.

❸ Keep in touch with both your acquisitions editor and your production editor. Let them know, both in writing and by telephone, any special requirements that your manuscript entails (for example, notations or terminology with which the copy editor might be unfamiliar). Ask about the next step in the process and when you should expect to hear from someone at the press. If you don't get a call, make sure you call to find out why.

❹ Make sure your likes and dislikes are known. If you hate green, let your editor know now, not after you've received an advance copy of your book with the cover done in chartreuse.

When Your Baby Comes Back as a Grown-Up

It's a jaded author who does not swell with pride upon seeing his or her book in print. *With justification.* Being published is an enormous accomplishment, and you should savor every moment of satisfaction.

Savor your book as well. Thumb through it. Smell the ink on its pages. Test the feel of it in your hands. This is your baby grown up, and you have every right to be proud.

Your production team is proud, too. They work in publishing because they love the written word and respect its power. When your book comes back to them, they savor the moment as well, believing that together, you and they have produced a work that will touch lives and affect ways of thinking and living, and perhaps even ways of being. This is no small matter.

And both of you are essential to the process. You, because you've labored long and hard to deliver your ideas well; the production team because they believe that your work is important enough to be read.

Summary

Although the production process can seem daunting to the uninitiated, most publishing companies follow the same basic steps. Once you know what these steps are and why they are important, the process proves to be logical and efficient. In just a few months, your complete manuscript journeys through production and emerges as a printed, bound book ready to be sold to the targeted audience. Let us now look at how you and your publisher can work together to market your book to that audience, and thus make sure as many copies as possible are sold.

9 | Marketing Your Book

You've made it through copyediting. You've seen the actual pages of your manuscript transformed into typed pages with all the art in the right place and in a format that makes your carefully written prose easier to read. You have even survived the tedious process of preparing the index for your book. The magic day comes when a box from your publisher arrives at your office with the first copy of your new book. Handsome, well written, adeptly edited, skillfully designed, and properly indexed. After the many months of hard work, you are ready to put up your feet and relax while the publisher promotes your book to the four corners of the globe.

Don't get too comfortable . . . at least, not yet. One of the mistakes that authors make with their books is to drop the ball once the book appears in print. After all, they reason, marketing is the publisher's job. Right? Well, only partially. Naturally, the publisher wants to sell as many copies of your book as possible and, if you researched your publisher properly, that publisher will be aggressive and competent in its promotional effort.

Nevertheless, while the publisher's interests lie with your own, it will be using the general methods found to be effective in selling all the books it publishes. If you want your book to receive a marketing push that is tailor-made to reach your readership, then you will need to help your publisher with your knowledge of your audience and your enthusiasm for the ideas contained in your book.

How Publishers Market Books

In the opening chapter we mentioned the different channels by which various publishers—trade, textbook, and specialty—promote their books. So you know something of what you can expect. If your book is with a scholarly publisher, now is *not* the time to demand your publisher send you on a book-signing tour or get you on "Geraldo." Because you already have a general idea of the types of marketing strategies your publishing house regularly uses, let's look at some of the promotional techniques publishers use in a little more detail.

Marketing Preparations

Promotion of your book will begin long before a copy ever arrives in your mailbox. Advance sales are important for publishers, both in helping determine long-term sales potential and in having a supply of cash already in the bank to help cover the up-front costs of production and printing. Many of these strategies will be invisible to you. The publisher will typically advise library wholesalers of the book, contact foreign subsidiaries, and attempt to sell foreign rights, translations, and book club rights. At the same time, the publisher might consult you on the advertising copy for catalog advertisements, the design of the cover, and names of people who might provide endorsements. Usually, you will be asked to fill out a marketing questionnaire, which will ask for specific marketing suggestions and information you have.

Catalog Advertisements

Publisher catalogs include groups of the publisher's books that fall into a specific category, such as "New This Year,"

"Spring 1994 Books," "Research Methods," and "Humanistic Psychology." These are mailed to lists drawn from associations, organizations, journals, or other book buyer lists the publisher either maintains or can obtain. Catalogs are also sent to relevant professional meetings.

Flyers

Generally smaller advertisements of your book, flyers often include an order blank and can be distributed at conventions or at any presentations you make before a group of people who might be interested in a book on your topic. Some publishers regularly prepare these one-book flyers for authors, while others will only do so on your request.

Publishers might also prepare multibook flyers to use in minimailings or to send to conferences. For example, if a publisher has three or four books on a specific topic, such as AIDS or the nutritional habits of athletes, a flyer will make a cost-effective method of promotion that can be mailed to a very targeted group.

Conventions

Publishers rent exhibit space at conventions and academic meetings to display their books to potential buyers. Because the cost of these booths is very high, publishers will usually buy booths only when they have a number of titles to display. Featured titles are often highlighted with a poster or other promotional device. Even if the publisher does not provide a full booth at a specific meeting, it will often send copies of your book or flyers to a combined exhibit of publishers if it believes it can gain some sales or promotional benefit.

Advertisements

Some publishers also regularly purchase advertising space inside convention programs and various journals to promote your book. This method is generally more effective for getting name recognition for your book rather than generating actual sales. Don't make the mistake of measuring your publisher's commitment to your book by the amount of advertising it negotiates. Because such ads might be expensive and do not result in specific sales, the publisher could well find it more productive to put that money into other efforts.

Review Copies

Your publisher will have a bank of addresses of media who are likely to review your book. Depending upon the press and the book, the publisher might attempt to reach public media like national and regional newspapers, magazines, and literary reviews. For any scholarly book, it will certainly attempt to obtain reviews in the major journals in your field. The publisher could also try to "seed the clouds" by distributing free copies to well-known figures in your discipline, or teachers who are likely to adopt your book for their classes.

Other Sales Mechanisms

In addition to the above strategies, different types of publishers might use several other approaches to sell their books. Remember, we discussed the various types of publishers—trade, text, and scholarly—in Chapter 1. Do not assume that the sales techniques that work in one category of publishing will work effectively and efficiently in another type.

Sales Representatives

College textbook publishers generally have sales representatives who call directly on those people who can make a decision to buy multiple copies of your book, such as college professors and bookstore managers. Sales reps are most effective in generating multiple-copy sales of your book. Because these decisions often mean dozens or hundreds of copies sold, large textbook publishers want a personal representative pushing their products directly to the decision maker.

On the other hand, sales reps are an unnecessary luxury for scholarly publishers, who generally sell most copies of their books to individuals. Even if their books are used as texts in advanced courses, the instructors for such courses can be reached through direct mail more economically than by sales reps.

Sample or Complimentary Copies

A textbook publisher will give free copies of your book away to instructors who teach a course in your subject area, in the hope that they will select your book for their course. The number of copies of your book that the publisher's sales reps are allowed or encouraged to "sample" is often an indicator of the publisher's commitment to the project.

Do not use this indicator for scholarly publishers, however. Scholarly publishers seldom give many book samples away. Remember the economic model of a scholarly monograph in Chapter 1? With a print run of 1,000 to 1,500 copies, the publisher cannot afford to give too many away, although most do have "exam" policies, in which a professor may request a copy of a book to examine for possible use in a course. The professor then has the option of returning the copy, buying it for his or her personal library, or keeping it as a desk copy if it is adopted for the course.

Telemarketing

Some publishers (including some scholarly publishers) use telemarketing to contact potential buyers or follow up on people who have requested a sample copy of your book. Sales reps might also phone people who teach a course on your book's topic, or who appear on a mailing list in your book's area.

Trade publishers, in need of getting attention for your book on crowded bookstore shelves and announcing your book to a broader audience of people, use a different set of strategies. Like textbook publishers, they will have a network of sales representatives calling on bookstores, hoping to convince the store (or chain) buyer that they should carry your book. They also employ the following techniques:

Media Press Releases. Publicity departments within a trade publishing house will prepare news stories about your book (or you) for use in newspapers and on radio and television shows. This strategy is effective for getting people to recognize your book, and sometimes it helps generate requests for your book at bookstores. It is less common in scholarly publishing, unless your book happens to correspond to some other newsworthy event; for example, a book on the downfall of the Soviet Union just when the Baltic states announce their independence.

Interviews. Your publisher can help arrange a speaking tour for you to be interviewed on the radio or television and for book signings at bookstores. While very effective for trade books, interviews are rarely productive at selling books for the scholarly or text markets, and few scholarly publishers have the resources to support such a high-profile speaking tour.

As noted, it is important to remember that these techniques do not work for all types of publishers. Whether trade, text, or scholarly, publishers employ promotional methods that are most effective for their product. To insist that your publisher send out hundreds of sample copies of your scholarly book or send media releases to, say, all northeastern newspapers will do little to endear you to your promotion manager or to encourage sales of your book. There are, however, some things you can do that will accomplish both these goals.

How You Can Help

A good book will not sell without the help of an effective marketing campaign. Word of mouth is too slow a process, and your book will be out of print before the news of your volume has spread beyond friends of your co-workers and associates. And no representative of any publisher—marketing director, promotion manager, or sales representative— knows more or cares more about the success of your book than you do. To rely exclusively on the publisher's marketing and sales force to sell your book is to ignore this secret, potent sales force—you.

While your publisher does not expect you to walk around the quad of your campus, wearing a sandwich board advertising your book (although we do know of one author who did just that), a combined sales effort between you and your publisher is more effective than either working alone. In this spirit of partnership, good communication, coordination, and information sharing are crucial. And, because the promotion manager may be responsible for promoting a dozen (or a hundred) books at one time, much of the onus of coordinating the activities falls on you. So get your feet off the desk, there's work to do—that is, if you want your book out of your publisher's warehouse and into the hands of the people for whom you wrote it.

Communicate With the Marketing Department Directly. Besides your editor, the most important person you need to know to help your book's sales is your promotion manager. We have already suggested that you should get to know him or her. Call on the phone and try to meet at conventions. Find out what the promotion manager knows about your book and its market and what kind of information you can supply that will help sell your book more productively. For example, make sure he or she understands the theme of your book and what makes it unique.

Target your specific readership when you develop marketing suggestions for your publisher. You already included information on the specific audience for your book in your proposal. Now is the time to remind your editor and promotion manager about that information and also any additional information you might have gathered since then. The more you and your publisher share ideas about the marketing of your book, the more your book is likely to sell.

Learn the Marketing Plan. Now is the time to learn about the publisher's marketing plan for your book. As you have discovered throughout the publishing process, the best way of finding out is by asking questions. So don't hesitate to ask the promotion manager, marketing director, or your editor for a copy of the plans, if they are in writing, or a description of them if they are not. Ask about:

- their draft advertising copy
- their list of review journals
- the list of publications in which they plan to place ads
- the materials given to the sales force
- the list of conventions at which they plan to show your book

If you don't already know, find out if they have ever published a book in this area before, how that sold, and what techniques they used to promote it. Ask to whom they will be sending catalogs and flyers and where they got the names. Likewise, find out how often an ad or catalog on your book will be mailed in the first and second years, and how long it will be promoted.

Offer Your Help. With a clear idea of the publisher's plans for marketing your book, you can begin to supplement those efforts with your own. Your help will be appreciated. And when you like a particular job that the publisher has done, drop a line saying "thanks." Praise from an author has often helped spur a marketing department to put additional effort into promoting a book—in this case, yours.

A brief warning, however: Nothing pushes a marketing department's "deaf button" faster than an author's claim that his or her book will sell everywhere. A few dictionaries, and possibly the Bible, have reached that lofty state, but they are the exceptions that prove the rule: No book sells everywhere. If you have written a scholarly monograph or a text for a specific course, it is highly unlikely that one of the chain bookstores will be interested in selling it next to the latest James Michener or Anne Tyler novel.

Teach the Marketing Staff About Your Book. You know it better than they ever will, so make sure they know why it's important and why you think readers will want to buy it. Specific members of the marketing and sales staff require different type of information:

For the *promotion manager,* describe the abilities of your reader: Do your readers need any particular course knowledge to understand your book? Have they had any specific training that would make them more interested in a book on this topic? What topics in the subject area of your book are most likely to interest your readers?

For the *promotion manager* or *copywriter:* Are there particular features of your book that would be most interesting to your reader? Are there any terms that are buzzwords in your field that should appear early in the ad? What tone should an ad have? Can your readers be offended by the use of too much hype or by the use of adverbs and adjectives? Would an endorsement by a particular person be influential in getting your readers to look at your book?

You might also point out particularly resonant passages in your book, develop a list of the strengths and weaknesses of the books that compete with your own book, or create a list of the concepts that instructors most often read before deciding on a textbook, and list the page numbers and paragraphs where you provide a particularly clear explanation.

Aid in Implementing the Publisher's Marketing Plan. While much of the activity goes on within the press, you can do many things to make sure the publisher gets the most out of the marketing campaign it is launching for your book:

Marketing questionnaire: The publisher will send you a questionnaire for your suggestions for marketing the book. Take it seriously and provide as much information as you can. Do the research to get the addresses of contact people and the names of those specialized journals. Contact the people who can give you testimonials.

Mailing lists: Publishers who sell primarily through direct mail live and die by the quality of the mailing lists they can obtain. While the publisher might have a general idea of the audience for your book, you are more likely to know the targeted networks. And the more targeted the direct-mail campaign, the less money wasted on people not interested in your book, and the more money that will be available to sell your book to real potential buyers. So become a mailing list scout for your publisher—subscriber lists to newsletters and journals to which you subscribe, contacts for your local research institute, directories of small organizations to which you belong. All of these will be invaluable to the publisher, no matter what the size of the list. If you can obtain the list for the publisher (preferably at no cost), or provide the name and address of a contact person, the publisher is more likely to follow up.

Similarly, whenever you go to a conference attended by people who would be interested in your book, try to pick up the address list (sometimes via the program) of all those who attended. Remember: No conference is too small. Regardless of the number of people who attended the conference, the mailing list can be useful for promoting your book. In fact, some of the very small conferences can be targeted specifically for your book. For a book on rural elderly, a list from a small conference of 115 people on rural social services could produce more results, and certainly would be more cost-efficient, than a large mailing to the National Association of Social Workers.

Conventions: Arrange to be a speaker or to lead a workshop on your book's topic at as many conventions as possible. For your book on qualitative research methods in aging, you could develop talks for major national conferences in gerontology as well as regional meetings. In addition, you could speak at conventions related to qualitative research. Use parts of your book's theme for your speaking engagements for the year prior to and the year after publication. If you have edited a book, you might be able to get several of the contributors together to present a session at a convention. For example, the contributors of a book on midlife loss organized a session on that topic at a national conference, resulting in multiple sales of the book. In any case, make sure the publisher knows your speaking schedule.

If your publisher is not attending a particular conference, ask your promotion manager to provide you with flyers that you can have available to distribute at your talk or put on a literature table. Some authors include order forms in their handouts or even ask the convention coordinator to include it in the convention package. If all this seems too "direct" for you, try to get the person who introduces your talk to give a plug for your book. If you are a featured speaker, your publisher might even be willing to host a small reception in your honor.

These sales techniques are well within scholarly norms and often bring impressive results. We have seen publishers' booths absolutely jammed with people wanting to buy a particular book after the author has given a talk on his or her book's subject. For example, a recent book was published the day before our author was to give a keynote address at a major conference. A large box of books was shipped to the conference, but it was not nearly enough to meet the demand of readers who flocked to the booth after the author's speech. Sales that day doubled the prepublication sales that had taken months to generate.

Bulk sales: Last but not least, keep your eye open for any groups that might be interested in buying bulk quantities of your book and give their names to your publisher. Most publishers will be happy to try to arrange a substantial discount for a large order.

Engage in Independent Activities. The publisher is never able to do it all, because there is no end to the number of marketing activities that can be undertaken to promote a book. When you discover the limits of your publisher's reach, it will be up to you to supplement them, keeping the publisher advised so that it can support you with whatever materials you need. Some of the more common author-initiated strategies are:

Working with university public relations offices: Most universities actively encourage their professors to write. And most have public relations offices to promote the activities of the faculty. Find out if your institution has a publicity department that can generate a media release for your book. We recently had an author who sent some of the media releases to his promotion manager, who then included them in complimentary copies going out to journal book reviewers. Reviewers responded with timely reviews. Another book in this series, *Working With the Media,* contains more detailed information on working with the university public relations office.

Contacting your campus bookstore: Many university bookstores have a "Faculty Corner" for their university authors. Make sure they know about your book, and give them the information they need to order some copies. And of course, make sure your librarian knows why your book needs to be in the university and department libraries. Finally, see if your institutional newspaper or faculty newsletter will interview you or review your book.

Making local appearances: Although your scholarly publisher is not going to actively sell to bookstores, you might be able to get your local bookstores to take a few copies. This could be especially effective if your book is on a topic of local interest, or if the bookstore has a section devoted to local authors. A local book signing can often be a big ego boost and sell copies of the book. Publishers will usually cooperate with these local efforts. In addition, some scholarly publishers might be willing to target specialty bookstores, such as sports bookstores or feminist bookstores, so send along the names of any specialty bookstores related to your topic.

Sending out your own flyers: Ask for a stack of flyers from your publisher. Put them in department mailboxes, give one to your dean, include them in your correspondence, take them with you on speaking engagements and other professional travel.

Summary

Just as producing your book was a joint endeavor, so is marketing your book a partnership. By taking the steps suggested in this chapter, you can help your book sell much more effectively than it would have otherwise. Find out how the marketing department plans to promote your book, and work with the staff to tailor their efforts to your book. In addition, the best, most knowledgeable, most caring salesperson for your book is you. Your own activities can do as much as anything the publisher can provide for you.

After putting all that work into your manuscript, why not take the additional time to make sure it sells? You might not become rich, but your book will be widely read by those for whom you wrote it. And what better reason is there to write than to know that your research and your ideas are being disseminated and possibly advancing your field?

10 | Twenty Common Publishing Problems and How to Solve Them

Over the years of our collective experience, we've discovered that the kinds of problems authors face with publishers are recurring ones. Thus, in the spirit of the troubleshooting automotive or computer manual, we provide this troubleshooting guide to 20 of the most common publishing problems you are likely to encounter in getting your book published.

Finding the Right Publisher

1. *You mailed your proposal/manuscript and weeks go by without a response.* This is not always bad news. Manuscripts that are clearly inappropriate for the publishing house are usually recycled back to the author fairly quickly. But your response is simple—call and ask. This will get you directly in touch with the acquisitions editor who is considering your book and allow you an opportunity to convince him or her of its applicability to the press's list. It will also allow you to ask for a schedule for considering your proposal, including an appropriate time for you to call back to see how the process is coming along.

2. The publisher wants exclusive rights to consider the book.
The good news is that they're definitely interested; the bad
news is that you are being asked to stall the other six publishers to whom you sent your material. This is certainly their
right, but is only in your best interests if this is your first choice
of publisher. If it is, and if you are willing to wait several
months for their answer, do so; however, try to limit their
"exclusive" to 60-90 days. This will force them to be expedi-
tious in getting you an answer. If the publisher is not your
first choice, you might wish to refuse their request. You could
consider using that request to let the publisher who *is* your
first choice know that other publishers are interested.

*3. You receive letters of interest from several publishers. Can you
negotiate with several simultaneously?* Cooperate with all of
them; this is the beauty of a free market economy. Let each
know that other publishers are also reviewing your proposal.
This validates their own interest in the project and should
force them to work faster and try harder to get you a contract.
Speak with all the interested publishers regularly and ask lots
of questions about what they would do with the book.

An anthropologist friend recently submitted a manuscript
to a university press on *Images of the Body*. The press sat on it
for 6 months, then politely rejected it. The second time around,
she sent it to a dozen other university presses. Nine wrote
back within the ensuing month, expressing some interest. After
informing all nine that other publishers were interested, she
focused on the two who had responded most quickly and
enthusiastically. At last word, she was considering which of
the two contracts to sign.

Contract Negotiations

*4. You have one contract in hand, but several other interested
publishers have indicated they might come through with contracts.*
Not an unpleasant position to be in. Having offered you a

contract, the first publisher is still likely to want the book a month from now. If you delay signing for a few weeks, the publisher is not likely to change its mind. And having a contract in hand is leverage to get the other publishers to move more quickly if they really want the project.

5. Now you have two, or three, or five contracts in hand. How do you decide which one to sign? Obviously, you want to pick the best offer. The trick is knowing what makes one offer better than the others. Remember, the best offer is not always the one with the highest royalties or best advances. Review your goals for the book (see Chapter 3), and ask the publishers lots of questions about how they can meet those goals. Then list the publishers in order of priority. If your best offer is weak in some areas, you should have the leverage to extract some promises (in writing, of course) to meet your concerns in exchange for signing their contract. For example, you might want to ask for a clause stipulating that the book will be published within a reasonable time frame.

6. The contract has a lot of "whereases" and "hereinafters." You don't understand some of the legal mumbo jumbo. Ask the acquisitions editor or contracts administrator for an explanation of anything you don't understand. Ask how often the clause is invoked. Ask how the legal language relates to the publisher's standard practices. Don't stop until you are clear on what the legal language actually says, how it relates to the publisher's modus operandi and its implications for you and your book. It's the editor's job to answer these questions. It is also to the editor's benefit to make sure everything is clear from the beginning, rather than having to deal with "I didn't know that" problems later on. Remember, once you've signed, you are stuck with those terms.

7. You find some of the contract clauses unpalatable. Can you change them? Academic authors commonly find several clauses uncomfortable. For example, publishers regularly ask for the right of first refusal to your next book, regardless of whether they might be the most appropriate publisher for it in your eyes. Some publishers include a clause asking you to promise that you will not write a book that will compete in the market with the one you are writing for them. While it is reasonable to expect that you will not write competing introductory textbooks for different publishers, this clause is sometimes invoked for advanced-level books. Because most scholars work in the same subfield all their careers, very likely your next scholarly book will compete for market share with your current one.

Ask the publisher why the clause is there, and ask to have it removed if you don't like it. If the publisher has good reasons to retain it to cover *some specific* eventualities, ask that those limited conditions clarifying the contractual language be put in writing, either in the contract or in a letter from your acquiring editor.

8. The editor has made promises to you that are not in the contract. This is not unusual. Not every item relevant to your understanding about the book is in the contract. But if you want to be sure you get it, get it in writing from the editor *before* you sign the contract. Promissory and explanatory letters of this sort are as binding on the publisher as the contract. Keep these letters, along with the contract, in a safe place.

9. They're offering good royalties and a decent advance. How nice! Maybe. Make sure you know on what basis royalties are calculated, net or gross sales (see Chapter 1), and what the publisher typically charges against royalties (indexing, honoraria to contributors on edited books, corrections during proofreading, copyright permission fees). Ask the editor. Is the advance refundable? If so, you'll have to pay it back if the book doesn't generate enough royalties to cover the advance, or if the publisher doesn't accept the manuscript.

10. The publisher already has three books on the same topic as yours. Isn't this going to hurt your book? Not necessarily. In the case of advanced, professional books, having a number of books on the same topic allows the publisher to combine marketing budgets for these books and promote to the key audience more often. In textbooks, the publisher wants a "new" item for a particular course each year. So if your introductory psychology book is scheduled against the seventh edition of their existing intro text, then your book won't get much play. On the other hand, if it is scheduled for the following year, it will get considerable attention as their new introductory psychology textbook for that season.

While Writing the Manuscript

11. As hard as you try, there is just too much to cover. The book is going to be longer than the pages you were given in the contract. Should you change the specs on your printer and hope for the best? Length is a ticklish question. Part of the editor's process of selling the book proposal to the publishing house included a financial analysis of potential sales, costs, and pricing. A change in the manuscript length will affect all of these, possibly making the book financially less appealing to the publisher. A supplementary text that was viable at $16.95 might not be at $24.95. So check with the editor to see what flexibility there is in this area. If there is none, ask for help in finding ways to cut. It might be a difficult process, but the resulting book is likely to be more focused and concise, a better book.

12. You're editing or coauthoring and the other parties aren't coming through. Is there anything the publisher can do to help? Responsiveness to your colleagues on your part, regular requests for progress reports from the other authors, and good interpersonal and motivational skills can usually do far more to keep the project moving along than publisher intervention. One good volume editor we know sends regular monthly progress reports to all the authors, highlighting promised delivery dates and the reality of what has actually arrived. This can sometimes shame slower authors into putting this project higher on their priority list.

The publisher usually prefers to serve as solution of last resort with coauthors or contributors, intervening only to patch up a troubled relationship that threatens to scuttle the project, or if the normal coauthorial process does not work.

13. Your relationship with your editor is not good. He or she is not responsive, and has different ideas than you have on where the book should go. A good relationship with your editor can often greatly improve the quality of the book. Conversely, a bad relationship can often lead to conflict and stress over the project. These problems can come from a variety of sources: interpersonal incompatibility, unresponsiveness on one or both sides, second thoughts (from either party) on the appropriateness of the book for the press. But before giving up on your editor as a lazy, ignorant boor, try several tactics:

a. Be responsive yourself. Answer requests from the editor quickly and fully.
b. Involve the editor in the project. Ask for feedback and take that feedback seriously.
c. Talk it out. Misunderstandings do occur, and the editor, who could be dealing with 50 or 100 authors like yourself at any given time, might not know how he or she is coming across to you.
d. Find an intermediary—whether a series editor, another friend of yours with whom the editor has worked before, or the editor's boss or assistant. Someone you both trust might help pave the way to better relations.
e. Make sure you're working toward the same goal. If the focus of your book has changed, your editor might be fighting you because the new direction no longer fits the market niche for which he or she argued for its publication.

f. In the worst possible case, ask to be released from your contract. The editor doesn't want months or years of conflict or grief any more than you do.

14. *The publishing house that has the contract for your book was just bought by a media and fast-food conglomerate. What now?* Unfortunately, your contract probably contains a clause allowing the publisher to assign the contract to someone else (see Chapter 6). Few publishers will sign a contract with you without such an assignment clause, as their list of future contracts is their chief asset if they ever want to sell the company. So you have little legal recourse.

The experience might be beneficial, or it might be harmful to the production and promotion of your book. For example, if the new publisher bought your old publisher specifically to obtain your field, your book, your part of its list, then you can rest assured that the publisher will work hard to make sure your book gets all the attention it deserves. In addition, if your old publisher was sold because it was bankrupt, chances are that it was doing a poor job publishing and promoting its books. So, again, you will be better off with the new owners, once the dust has settled.

In other cases, the results might not be so fortuitous. Your contract could be canceled or sold as part of a list to yet a third party. Equally disastrous, you could even end up with an editor who knows nothing about your book and has little interest in learning.

What can you do? As soon as possible, find out who is in charge of the project at the new publisher. And, as often suggested elsewhere in this book, build a network of relationships within the new publishing house as quickly as possible. This will serve to differentiate your project from the dozen of other "faceless" ones the new publisher is trying to process.

We generally find that most authors see the process of change disconcerting at first. Nevertheless, once new relationships are forged, they discover that the new publisher is eager to work with them to ensure the success of their books.

If you remain unhappy with the new order, however, you can ask to be released from the contract, although this can be a risky strategy if the answer is "no." Recognize that it could be a frustrating experience. If the book is already in production or has already been published, try to be a squeaky wheel to get your share of attention, and do all you can to promote your own book.

15. *The editor sent your project out for review. The reviews came back contradictory. One reviewer didn't want you to change anything. One of the reviewers obviously didn't read the manuscript; Another obviously didn't understand it. Which set of reviews should you follow?* Reviewing is not a science; a review is one person's presumably educated opinion of another person's work. If the editor has selected a good set of reviewers, you should get useful, sympathetic feedback. But that doesn't always happen. Much of the problem can often be solved by your involvement in the editor's process of choosing reviewers and in negotiating what questions the reviewers are asked. Suggest a list of reviewers who would, in your estimation, provide fair, tough-minded advice. Also provide the editor with a list of people you feel would not review your manuscript fairly. And suggest the kinds of questions that would be useful for the reviewers to answer for *you*.

But if the reviews are contradictory, you'll need guidance. A good editor will send the reviews to you with suggestions on what to pay attention to and what to ignore. If the editor doesn't, your first task will be to write such a letter yourself— what you plan to change and what to ignore. If the editor accepts your plans for revision, he or she can't argue about it later on. Negotiate a revision strategy with the editor, clarify this strategy in writing, and then stick to it (see chapters 5 and 7).

The Production Process

16. *You submitted your manuscript several months ago, but in the last-minute haste of finishing the book, there are a couple of rough edges, citations you would like to add, paragraphs you would like to rework. Can you change what you've written?* Follow the maxim, "the sooner the better." While much of the production cycle time is actually taken with your manuscript waiting in a queue for its turn, as time goes by, designs, pages, and type get fixed and become harder and more expensive to change. Many publishers solve this "last pass through the manuscript" problem by providing authors with a copyedited manuscript to review and change as needed. This is also your opportunity to correct a bad job of copyediting. If your publisher regularly sends a copyedited manuscript, make sure you make *all* the changes you wish at that time. If the publisher doesn't, your first conversation with the production editor responsible should include an inquiry about the possibilities for substantive or bibliographic changes. Usually there is a window in the first few weeks after submitting the manuscript. But when the book is 24 hours away from the printer, you are likely to meet with a lot of resistance—to say the least.

17. *The production process is taking forever. How do you speed it up?* You can do little, other than be responsive when the publisher asks for information or proofreading from you. Being a squeaky wheel to the production department—or to your acquisitions editor—sometimes helps, but might backfire instead. You should know how long it takes to produce the book, based upon your conversations with the editor before you signed the contract. If it is proceeding much slower than that, you can do little other than monitor each step or ask your acquisitions editor to monitor it for you. Although some publishers include a contractual clause promising publication within a specified amount of time, most do not.

18. You're told you have to do an index. You've never done one before. You can do it yourself, hire an indexer, or ask the publisher to hire an indexer (usually at your expense). Should you elect to do it, many style guides and books on publishing have information on preparing an index (see Additional Resources section). Your publisher might be able to help you with some information. Off-the-shelf computer programs also exist. In spite of this, let's admit it: Preparing an index is difficult, tedious work. The book will be better for having a good index, but the burden of preparing a good index usually rests on you. One consolation, however: Thousands of authors before you were first-time indexers, and they succeeded. You can, too.

After Publication

19. Why aren't they marketing your book more aggressively? First, check to make sure this perception is correct. Many marketing activities are invisible ones—dealing with library wholesalers and abstracting services, sending review copies, negotiating foreign rights or book club sales, shipping copies to conferences that you might not attend. Ask the publisher for a list of marketing activities it has undertaken: catalogs that have displayed the book (ask for samples), a list of journals that have received review copies, a list of places where space advertisements have been placed, a list of conferences at which the book will be shown, a list of bookstores at which it has attempted to have the book stocked, and, for textbooks, a list of potential adopters who were given free copies.

With this list in hand, you can provide additional marketing suggestions on which the promotion manager can follow up. But, to do so, you will need to be realistic in your expectations ("Send copies to the book review editor of every paper in the country" is not realistic), focused in your demands (identify specific direct-mail targets, for example), and helpful in your demeanor. As much of the legwork that you can do in obtaining a mailing list or finding a contact for placing an ad will make the promotion manager's job that much easier. They will be more likely to follow up on your suggestions (see Chapter 9).

20. You know you are owed royalties. Where are they? All publishers' contracts should contain a provision on when they will provide an accounting and payment of royalties. If the date has passed, call the publisher—either the royalty department or the acquisitions editor. In some cases, computer glitches, lost records, or other human errors might have held up payment. In a few cases, the publisher is looking at that money as a free loan from you. Be firm. It is your money.

When you get a statement and check, contact the royalty department or your acquiring editor if you don't understand what the statement says or if there are charges against your royalties that you didn't expect. The publisher must provide an accurate accounting to you. Because these are the same accounts that it gives the IRS, it needs to be accurate. If the figures look incorrect, ask the publisher for other documentation of sales.

As for the few unscrupulous publishers who renege on their commitment to pay royalties, it is not without cost. One publisher we know went through a brief period of withholding royalties 20 years ago. And still today some scholars tell us, "I won't publish with Payless Press; they don't pay their royalties."

If there are any common themes in this guide, they are that, for all its imposing formal structure, publishing is a social activity. Good personal relations with the people at the publishing house can usually get you better treatment, as can close attention to the goings-on inside the black box. Your ideas are good ones, worthy of print. Build those relationships, learn the world that publishers inhabit, and those ideas are more likely to reach their public.

Conclusion

We have taken you from your first idea on what to write through researching the right publisher, preparing your proposal, getting your contract, working with your editor and other members of your publisher's staff, getting through production, and on to the final marketing of your book. Certain themes have emerged throughout the examination of each of these parts of the publishing process. The following is a list of the 10 most important lessons that we hope you take away from this book.

1. *Publishing Is a Business.* Publishing is not a charitable venture, and your book is not just words strung together on paper. Publishing is a business, and your book is a product to be sold to the appropriate customer. Once you learn to view publishing in this way, you can understand how your publisher looks at it. There is much idealism in the publishing business, but the bottom line, as with any other business, is that the product has to sell. If too many products don't sell, the publisher will be out of business.

2. *Sell Your Ideas.* Because publishing is a business, convincing publishers of the worth of your book is a selling job and must be approached as such. Your proposal must give

the editor enough information about the project, and its intended audience, for him or her to make a decision as to whether it is appropriate for the publisher and if it will be able to sell enough copies to warrant production and promotion investments. In addition to being complete, the proposal should be well organized, well written, and letter perfect, thus reflecting well on you as a prospective business partner. Likewise, throughout the review and writing process, remember to talk your project up to your editor, production editor, and promotion manager. These people are responsible for your book within the press. Sell them on your project, and the likelihood of its getting the proper attention is greatly increased.

3. *Do Your Homework.* Finding the right publisher takes research and effort. It just doesn't make sense to put the work into researching and writing your book and not the extra effort into making sure you sign with the right publisher for you. Later, take the time to do that little extra work to help promote your book.

4. *Persistence Pays Off.* Rejection by one or more publishers does not mean your book is unpublishable. If one publisher says "no," go to the next on your list. Publishers are plentiful, and each one has different goals and agendas. Likewise, there are a lot of editors, each with different ideas of what makes a good book. If you are persistent in pursuing your goal, you will find the right combination.

5. *Network and Communicate.* You are probably an old pro at networking by now. You network with your colleagues at other universities and at professional meetings. You also need to network with publishing people. Building a good relationship with various people at different presses will greatly increase your chances of publication. And building good relationships with various people within the press will help smooth the writing and production processes once the book is under contract.

6. Keep Focused on Your Goals. Again, publishing is a business, and a publisher won't always have your interests in mind. The publisher's bottom line is to make a profit from your book. You, on the other hand, might have vastly different goals—to get tenure, to disseminate your research to your colleagues, to finally have the perfect text for your organizational behavior course. Concentrate on what is important to you, and don't be afraid to speak up about it. Once again, communication comes into play. Discuss with your editor how you can work together to make sure both your goals and your publisher's goals can be met.

7. Create a Partnership. We have spoken a lot about this. A publishing agreement is a partnership between an author and a publisher. Cooperation produces the best possible book and gives it the best chance of selling well. You need to be flexible, but so does the publisher. You both need to work together.

8. A Little Knowledge Goes a Long Way. The more you know about what goes on inside the publishing house, the better able you are to influence various aspects of the production and marketing effort. Indeed, stay in communication with your editor, but remember to also get to know others at the press and get their input.

9. Your Job Never Ends. Because you are the most knowledgeable and caring agent for your book, your role in producing the book does not end with its actual printing. Your role in selling it remains as long as the book is in print. And if you work on that role, your book will stay in print much longer.

10. Make It Fun. Whatever kind of writing you do, whether it is scholarly or trade, you are not likely to get rich or famous. So you might as well at least enjoy the process. Do whatever is best for you to enhance the enjoyment of actually sitting down and creating the written text. And make friends with your editor and others at the publishing house. It's always more enjoyable to work with a close friend than with a distant business acquaintance.

Keep these lessons in mind, and we are confident that you will be as enthusiastic about *your* end of publishing as we are about *our* end. And publishing is something we all should be enthusiastic about. The right to disseminate knowledge is a basic right in any free society, and that dissemination forever expands the horizon of civilization. So here's to seeing your book in print, to seeing it read far and wide, and to seeing it make an impact on the way we live. That is something that unites both author and publisher.

Appendix

August 29, 1992

Terry Hendrix, Senior Editor
Sage Publications, Inc.
2455 Teller Road
Newbury Park, CA 91320

Dear Terry,

I enjoyed meeting you at the International Communication Association meeting last month. I appreciated your taking the time to discuss my project. The resulting proposal for *Getting Your Book Published* is enclosed.

As an editor for a scholarly publisher, how many proposals do you reject each year? How many of those were rejected because the topic was inappropriate for a book? How many were from new academics eager for you to publish their dissertations? How many proposals were so poorly presented that you lost interest in trying to decipher the actual subject?

Quite simply, many scholars do not know how to go about submitting a proposal that is well executed and on an appropriate topic. In *Getting Your Book Published* we clearly explain the process by which an author can decide on a pertinent subject and write an effective book proposal. In so doing, we describe publishing as a business and the proposal as a selling tool.

As I mentioned when we met, the book will be jointly written by members of the editorial staff at our publishing house. Altogether, the authors have more than 50 years of publishing experience. We thus have the expertise necessary to write such a book.

In addition to the proposal, I am enclosing a sample chapter (The Review Process) and a list of possible reviewers. Should you have any questions, don't hesitate to call. Our telephone and fax numbers are listed below. We look forward to hearing from you and to the possibility of working with you on this project.

Sincerely,

Christine S. Smedley
Editor

Book Proposal

Getting Your Book Published by Christine S. Smedley, Mitchell Allen, Harry Briggs, Nancy S. Hale, Claudia Hoffman, and C. Deborah Laughton.

About This Project

Rationale

The editorial staff at Sage Publications, Inc., proposes to write a book detailing the process by which a potential author can get a scholarly book published. Most academics, at some point in their career, consider writing a book; indeed, many are required to write in order to secure tenure. Years of reviewing book proposals and talking to hopeful authors have convinced us that many scholars know little about what the publishing operation entails and what they can do to ensure that their book will be accepted and published. *Getting Your Book Published* will demystify this process and furnish authors with guidelines for finding the right publisher, writing a book proposal, and responding to reviews.

Coverage

In *Getting Your Book Published* we will clearly and concisely explain the process by which an author can decide upon a topic, write an effective book proposal, respond to reviews, and secure a contract. In addition, we will explain the parts of a contract, delineate the production process, and illustrate methods of book promotion.

Furthermore, the book will highlight publishing as a business, a partnership between author and publisher, and a social endeavor. Because it will focus primarily on scholarly publishing, we will not elaborate upon some of the specific aspects of either text or trade publishing.

Competing Works

Although numerous books describe publishing, few concentrate on scholarly publishing. For example, *How to Get Happily Published:*

A Complete and Candid Guide, by Appelbaum and Evans, covers many types of publishing, including self-publishing. As a result, the typical scholarly author must wade through many pages of irrelevant discussions to glean any advice relevant to his or her needs. Similarly, although *Handbook for Academic Authors*, by Luey, concentrates on issues relevant to the scholarly writer, it devotes an extremely lengthy discussion to each topic. On the cther hand, *Getting Your Book Published* is concise, specifically tailored to the needs of an overworked academic.

Specifications

We anticipate that the book will be approximately 150 manuscript pages. Some chapters may include one or two tables or figures, for which we will supply camera-ready art. In addition, we plan to include a sample proposal and cover letter as well as other relevant sample material. We do not anticipate needing a reference section, although we will incorporate a list of resources, including books and organizations, that we believe will be helpful to the prospective author.

The volume should fit well in Sage's new series, "Survival Skills for Scholars." It will be similar in length, tone, and complexity to Sage's recently published *Coping With Faculty Stress*, by Gmelch, and *Effective Committee Service*, by Smelser. The topic—helping an academic get published—makes this book an appropriate addition to the series.

Schedule

We anticipate having the first draft ready for review by February 1, 1993. A final draft will be ready for the publisher 2 months after the review process.

Authors

Getting Your Book Published will be jointly written by members of the editorial staff at Sage Publications. Collectively, we represent more than 50 years of publishing experience. We have worked with many different types of publishing houses—scholarly, text, and trade—and have held a variety of positions—editor, executive editor, sales representative, and director of marketing. In addition, we have been on the other side of the publisher/author relationship, as most of us have been through the process of submitting and getting published articles, short stories, and books. We thus have the experience and expertise essential for writing a book on scholarly publishing.

About the Market

Primary Audience

The main audience for *Getting Your Book Published* will be scholars who are interested in learning how to get published. Established academics as well as new scholars will find the information presented useful.

These scholars can be reached through many academic associations, such as the Gerontological Society of America and the International Communication Association. In fact, many of the associations to which Sage usually mails are appropriate sources for mailing lists. In addition, interested professors can be reached through lists obtained from CMG (College Marketing Group).

Secondary Audience

The volume could be used as a supplementary text in seminars on publishing and in university extension courses.

Outline

Introduction: Publishing 101

The introduction briefly describes what the book will specifically cover in each chapter and what we hope to accomplish in writing the book. We introduce ourselves as authors, demonstrating our expertise that qualifies us to write the book.

Chapter 1: The Business of Publishing

One of the facts of life prospective authors must face is that publishing is a business. This chapter covers publishing as a business, including a description of the different types of publishers and the basic economics of publishing. We stress that each type of publisher must make money to stay in business, and thus any publishing decision is essentially a business decision on whether to publish the book. We relate these facts to how the author must demonstrate to the publisher that his or her proposed book will be a good investment for the publisher.

Chapter 2: So You Want to Write a Book

How can a prospective author decide whether an idea is the germ of a book that a publisher will be interested in, or perhaps only worthy of a journal article? In this chapter we will examine what makes a book. We will also cover the issues of publishing a dissertation, and authoring or editing a book. Finally, we will give some tips on how one can actually get down to the business of writing.

Chapter 3: Finding the Right Publisher

One of the main problems in getting published is finding the appropriate publisher for a book. We will consider steps by which the author can find the right publisher—one that publishes books in the author's specific area, that promotes books to the appropriate market, and that satisfies the goals the author has in writing. In addition, we will cover such topics as when to first contact a publisher and whether an agent is necessary.

Chapter 4: Preparing a Book Prospectus

Developing an effective book proposal is the most important step in getting a contract. In this chapter we will examine what makes a quality proposal. We will cover the major parts of a proposal—the intellectual contribution, market potential, book specifications, author qualifications, and proposed outline.

Chapter 5: The Review Process

Once an author sends a proposal to the publisher, it undergoes extensive review, first by the editor and then through peer review.

In this chapter, we will cover the review process, what the reviews mean, and how the publisher uses them to make the decision whether to publish. In addition, we will suggest how the author can benefit from the reviews, even if they are negative.

Chapter 6: The Publishing Contract

Hopefully, the review process will lead to a contract offer. In this chapter we examine the various sections of a standard book publishing contract. We look at what rights the publisher expects to obtain, what rights the author retains, and what royalties the publisher is offering. We also discuss what parts of a contract are negotiable.

Chapter 7: Getting the Most Out of Your Editor

Even though the author now has a contract, most new authors know little about what to expect next. The following chapters will fill in this blank. First, we will explain what an author can expect from an editor and how the editor can help the author develop his or her manuscript, guide it through production, and ensure effective marketing. In addition, we will both argue that the world need not end if the author's editor leaves the publishing house, and recommend steps the author can take to minimize any negative effects.

Chapter 8: The Production Process

In this chapter we will explain the process of how a manuscript moves through production and emerges a bound book. We will emphasize what is expected of the author during this process and what the author can do to avoid or lessen production difficulties.

Chapter 9: Marketing Your Book

Here we give a realistic assessment of what an author can expect from a scholarly publisher in terms of marketing. We will also specifically suggest steps the author can take to help promote his or her own book.

Chapter 10: Twenty Common Publishing Problems and How to Solve Them

In any business, including publishing, things can go wrong. In this chapter we cover some common problems most often faced by authors and recommend methods for overcoming these problems.

Conclusion

Finally, we will briefly review what we consider to be the main themes of the book: First and foremost, publishing is a business. Thus the author must sell his or her project to the publisher as a solid business venture. Second, publishing is a partnership between the author and publisher, and the best books are a result of that partnership. Third, the best way to ensure a book is published and promoted properly is be in close communication with the editor and other members of the publishing team.

Additional Resources

Books

American Association of University Presses. (1977). *One book/five ways: The publishing procedures of five university presses*. New York: William Kaufman. Report of an experiment on how five different university presses handled the same proposed manuscript.

American Association of University Presses. (1992-1993). *American Association of University Presses directory, 1992-93*. A wealth of information on personnel, policies, and interests of various university presses.

(Author). (Annual). *Literary market place*. New Providence, NJ: R. R. Bowker.

(Author). (1969). *A manual of style* (12th ed.). (pp 399-430). Chicago: University of Chicago Press. A clear explanation of how to do an index.

Coser, L. A., Kadushin, C., & Powell, W. W. (1982). *Books: The culture and commerce of publishing*. New York: Basic Books. The major sociological study of the book publishing business.

Harmon, E., & Montagnes, I. (1987). *The thesis and the book*. Toronto: University of Toronto Press. Covers the process of turning a disseration into a book.

Larson, M. (1985). *How to write a book proposal*. Cincinnati, OH: Writer's Digest Books. Describes the various parts of a proposal for nonfiction books and why they are important components of a selling tool.

Luey, B. (1987). *Handbook for academic authors*. New York: Cambridge University Press. Covers various types of writing, from journal articles to dissertations, and the mechanics of publishing.

Miller, C., & Swift, K. (1988). *The handbook of nonsexist writing: For writers, editors and speakers*. New York: Harper & Row. Gives suggestions on how to avoid sexist language.

136

Parsons, P. (1989). *Getting published*. Knoxville: University of Tennessee Press. A description of university press publishing, including a list of which presses publish in which fields.

Perrin, P. G. (1959). *Writer's guide and index to english* (3rd ed.). Chicago: Scott, Foresman. Old but detailed description of English in a framework of practice in composition.

Porter, R. E., Gould, A. F., Gould, A. Sr., Dierks, J. C., Burnside, B. B., Burnside, W. R., Cassidy, M., Han, F., Hayes, C. F., Hungerford, L., Miller, D., Springer, M. (1979). *The writer's manual*. Palm Springs, CA: ETC Publications. Covers the mechanics of writing and getting published in a variety of formats—trade fiction and nonfiction, scripts, articles, and academic writing.

Powell, W. W. (1985). *Getting into print*. Chicago: University of Chicago Press. Superb ethnographic study of editorial decision making in two scholarly presses.

Strunk, W., Jr., & White, E. B. (1959). *The elements of style*. New York: Macmillan. A succinct book enumerating rules and principles for clear, concise writing.

Articles

Recent issues of *Publisher's Weekly* (published weekly by R. R. Bowker) and *Scholarly Publishing* (published quarterly by the Society for Scholarly Publishing).

Organizations

American Association of University Presses
One Park Avenue
New York, NY 10016

American Society of Indexers
1700 18th Street, NW
Washington, DC 20009

Independent Literary Agents Association
55 Fifth Avenue
New York, NY 10003

Society for Author Representatives
39-½ Washington Square, South
New York, NY 10012

About the Authors

Christine S. Smedley is the Editor for Nursing Health Sciences and Gerontology at Sage Publications, Inc., where she has worked for 7 years. Prior to entering the publishing field, Christine taught college-level freshman composition. She has several published articles to her credit. In her spare time she writes and does some developmental editing.

Mitchell Allen is Executive Editor for Sage Publications, responsible for acquiring books in sociology, anthropology, and other social sciences. He has worked for Sage, doing editorial acquisitions and marketing, since 1976 and has been responsible for the publication of more than 500 books. Mitch has offered workshops on book publishing at universities and professional conferences for more than a decade. In his other life, as a Near Eastern archaeologist, he has given conference presentations, published professional papers, and is preparing a book based on his archaeological survey project near Ashkelon, Israel.

Harry Briggs currently serves as Editorial Director of Sage Publications, Inc. He previously held posts as an acquisitions editor with Sage, National Textbook Company, and D. C. Heath and Company. Like many in the editorial profession, he began his publishing career with a stint as a college sales representative and regional sales manager while with D. C. Heath and Company.

Nancy S. Hale received a master's degree in English from Pepperdine University, where she also taught undergraduate English composition students. Her article on T. S. Eliot's dramatic theory appeared in *Student Writing Across the Disciplines,* edited by Clegg and Wheeler. She has worked in publishing for 3 years, serving as a contracts and rights/permissions assistant before her current role as Editorial Assistant at Sage Publications. Her future publishing plans include developmental editing and journalism.

Claudia A. Hoffman has been Graphics Production Manager, Managing Editor of the Journals Division, and Director of the Newsletters Division, and Managing Editor of the Books Division for Sage Publications, Inc.

C. Deborah Laughton began her publishing career as a sales representative with Wadsworth Publishing. She was a textbook acquisitions editor in the field of psychology and social science statistics for Brooks/Cole Publishing for 10 years, and has been the Acquisitions Editor in the area of research methods and psychology for Sage Publications, Inc., for the past 5 years. She has published short stories and essays and has written documentary segments for PBS's *Caseworks.*